VINTAGE
HIND SWARAJ

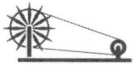

M.K. Gandhi was born in 1869 in Porbandar, India. He studied law in London and was admitted to the Inner Temple in 1891. He worked to improve the rights of immigrant Indians in South Africa and returned to India in 1915 to take up the struggle for independence from Britain. Gandhi never wavered in his belief in non-violent protests, and in 1947, he succeeded in uniting India with a national movement. In January 1948, Gandhi was assassinated as he walked to take part in his evening prayers.

Dhananjay Rai teaches at the Department of Gandhian Thought and Peace Studies, Central University of Gujarat. *Poorna Swaraj, Constructive Programme: Its Meaning and Place* (2023) is his most recent work.

Swaraj Special Number"; Gandhi sends *A Message to the Aryan Path*; bans lifted from *Hind Swaraj*.

1939 Revised new edition (revised of 1938 Edition); *Hind Swaraj or Indian Home Rule*; Preface to the New Edition by Mahadev Desai; An Important Publication [comment on the Aryan Path content], The Attack on Machinery and Civilisation, Limitations of the Doctrine, Preface by Mahadev Desai (1938); "A Word of Explanation" (rephrased title for *Hind Swaraj or The Indian Home Rule* by M.K. Gandhi (published in *Young India*, 26 January 1921); commences fast at Rajkot; World War II begins (and ends in 1945).

1940 "Gandhiji's Speech at the A.I.C.C." (15 September, *Harijan*); *An Autobiography or the Story of My Experiments with Truth* (translated from the original in Gujarati by Mahadev Desai) [this is the second edition by a combination of 1927 and 1929 volumes of *The Story* or *My Experiments with Truth*].

1941 Publishes *Constructive Programme: Its Meaning and Place*.

1942 The Quit India Movement; arrest and imprisonment in the Aga Khan Palace.

1945 The second edition of *Constructive Programme: Its Meaning and Place*.

1946 *The Gospel of Selfless Action,* or *the Gita according to Gandhi* (editor Mahadev Desai gives additional introduction and commentary to this translation of the original in Gujarati, published by Navajivan, Ahmedabad); *"Independence"* (28 July, *Harijan*, p. 236): Gandhi uses the well-known concept of the oceanic circle, envisioning a structure based on "ever-widening,

HIND SWARAJ

Introduced *with* notes *by*
DHANANJAY RAI

M.K. GANDHI

VINTAGE
An imprint of Penguin Random House

VINTAGE

Vintage is an imprint of the Penguin Random House group of companies
whose addresses can be found at global.penguinrandomhouse.com

Published by Penguin Random House India Pvt. Ltd
4th Floor, Capital Tower 1, MG Road,
Gurugram 122 002, Haryana, India

First published in Vintage by Penguin Random House India 2024

ISBN 9780143466017

Typeset in Adobe Garamond Pro by MAP Systems, Bengaluru, India
Printed at Manipal Technologies Limited, Manipal

www.penguin.co.in

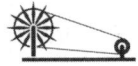

CONTENTS

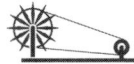

CHRONOLOGICAL INTERLOCUTORS

1600 Formation of the East India Company.

1652 Dutch land occupancy in South Africa begins.

1757 The East India Company wins in the Battle of Plassey.

1764 The Battle of Baxur takes place.

1765 The Treaty of Allahabad is signed and the East India Company acquires *Diwani* Rights.

1795 The beginning of the control of land by England in South Africa.

1805 Giuseppe Mazzini (1805–72); *Duties of Men* (1862) as a follow-up reading in *Hind Swarajya* (1909)/*Indian Home Rule/Hind Swaraj* (1910) [hereafter "as a follow-up reading"].

1817 Henry David Thoreau (1817–62); *On the Duty of Civil Disobedience* (1849) and *Life Without Principle* (1863) as follow-up readings.

1819 John Ruskin (1819–1900); *Unto This Last* (1862) and *Joy for Ever: And Its Price in the Market)* (1857) as follow-up readings.

1822 Henry Sumner Maine (1822–88); *Village-Communities in the East and West* (1871) as a follow-up reading.

1825 Dadabhai Naoroji (1825–1917): *Poverty and Un-British Rule in India* (1901) as a follow-up reading.

1828 Leo Tolstoy (1828–1910); *The Kingdom of God is Within You* (1894), *What is Art?* (1904), *The Slavery of Our Times* (1900), *The First Step: An Essay on the Morals of Diet* (1891), *How Shall We Escape (1898), A Letter to a Hindoo* (1908) as follow-up readings.

1844 Edward Carpenter (1844–1929); *Civilisation: Its Cause and Cure* (1889) as a follow-up reading.

1848 Romesh Chunder Dutt (1848–1909); *Economic History of India* (1902 and 1904) as a follow-up reading.

1849 Max Nordau (1849–1923); *The Conventional Lies of Civilization* (1883) and *Paradox* (1886) as follow-up readings.

1856 Annexation of Oudh.

1857 The Revolt of 1857; end of the Company Raj.

1858 The Government of India Act of 1858 marks the official start of the British Raj.

1859 Godfrey Blount (1859–1937); *New Crusade: An Appeal* (1903) as a follow-up reading.

1859 Authorization to let Indian indentured labourers into South Africa.

1861 Robert Sherard (1861–1943); *The White Slaves of England* (1897) as a follow-up reading.

1869 Birth of Mohandas Karamchand Gandhi on 2 October, Porbandar, Kathiawad, India.

1885 Burgher and property rights are prohibited, and Asians are required to register in South Africa.

1888 Gandhi joins the Inner Temple, Inn of Court, London.

1889 Sir William Wedderburn assumes the presidency of the recently formed British Committee of the Indian National Congress (London); commences *Journal India* 1900 onwards; Gandhi looks through *Song Celestial*, an English rendition of the Bhagavad Gita by Sir Edwin Arnold.

1891 Act 25 of 1891 deprives indentured labourers of citizenship in South Africa; Gandhi called to the Bar in London; Gandhi departs for India.

1893 Gandhi arrives in South Africa and encounters racism (refuses to remove turban in Durban Court; labelled as an "unwelcome guest" by *Natal Advertiser*; pushed off the train's first-class car at Pietermartizburg Station; hit by constable outside President Kruger's residence for walking on the pavement).

1894 *The Franchise Act of 1894* enables Natal to disenfranchise Indians; the beginning of Gandhi's engagement against disenfranchisement; petitions to institutions and individuals including Natal Legislative Assembly and Dadabhai Naoroji; foundation of Natal Indian Congress; Gandhi becomes its honorary secretary; admission to Natal Supreme Court; wins first case in South Africa defending Gope Maharaj; writes to Natal Legislators; Alfred John Webb (1834–1908), an Irish author and member of Parliament, becomes the president of the Indian National Congress. At the end of *Hind Swaraj*, Gandhi extracts contents from Webb's collection *The People of India: Their Many Merits. By Many Who Have Known Them* (1900) for the section "Testimonies by Eminent Men in Hind Swaraj"; studies Koran, Bible, Tolstoy's *The Kingdom of God is Within You*.

1895 A £3 tax imposed on ex-indentured labourers; Gandhi appeals to the Natal Assembly on re-indentured clause in Indian Immigration Bill; release of Balasundaram, an indentured labour; objection on tax on ex-indentured labour; Gandhi gets involved in the cause of the Indian Franchise; releases *The Indian Franchise: An Appeal to Every Briton in South Africa*.

1896 Disenfranchisement of Indians in Natal; Gandhi journeys to India and initiates a campaign advocating for the rights of Indians living in South Africa; prints *The Green Pamphlet* in Rajkot and then travels to Bombay, Madras, Poona and Calcutta; shares information regarding issues and matters that are of importance to the South African Indian community.

1897 Returns to South Africa; a crowd attacks him; Transvaal restricts marriage between whites and coloured people.

1900 Sends a draft resolution on the South African Indian problem to Dadabhai Naoroji for the Congress session.

1902 Moves a resolution on South Africa at Congress; returns to South Africa; leads delegation to Chamberlin.

1903 First edition of the *Indian Opinion*.

1904 Founding of "Phoenix Settlement" (Durban, Natal Province).

1905 Indians entering Transvaal require a permit, while Natal immigration is restricted.

1906 Commencement of satyagraha at the Empire Theatre in Johannesburg; the word "satyagraha" was chosen from Maganlal Gandhi's phrase "sadagraha"; Gandhi goes to England and then back to South Africa.

1907 Satyagraha against compulsory registration of Asians ("The Black Act"); publishes paraphrased eight out of fifteen chapters of *Ethical Religion* by William MacIntyre Salter in Gujarati in *Indian Opinion* (5 January 1907–23 February 1907). The Complete Works of Mahatma Gandhi (*CWMG*) VI contains English translation (273–76, 280–81, 284–87, 298–300, 312–13, 316–18, 330–32, 340–42). This was published as *Ethical Religion* by M.K. Gandhi in 1968 by Navajivan Trust, dealing with ideal morality, moral action, a higher law, morality as religion, religious morality or social, social ideal and personal morality.

1908 Plato (427–347 BCE). Gandhi reads his *Defence and Death of Socrates*; paraphrased and published Plato's *Apology* as *Ek Satyavirni Katha* (Story of A Soldier of Truth) in six issues of the *Indian Opinion*. The preface of *Story of A Soldier of Truth* was published on 4 April 1908. A follow-up reading suggested in *Hind Swarajya* (1909); Gandhi is on trial for inciting satyagraha and sentenced to two months in Johannesburg Prison (the first incarceration).

1909 The arrest of Gandhi and subsequent three months imprisonment in Transvaal for failing to produce a registration certificate; "Letter to Manilal Gandhi" (25 March 1909) to praise *Kingdom* as the most logical book and Tolstoy for the synthesis between practices and preachings; left with Haji

Habib on deputation for the Indian cause for England from South Africa on 21 June 1909; reaches London on 10 July 1909; communicates with Leo Tolstoy about satyagraha/ passive resistance; not successful with Transvaal laws; replies to Tolstoy and sends Doke's written biography to him; "Letter to H.S. Polak"(14 October 1909, London); leaves England on 13 November 1909; works on *A Letter to a Hindoo* (the first and second prefaces to *A Letter to a Hindoo*) and *Hind Swarajya* together on board S.S. Kildonan Castle; reaches South Africa on 30 November 1909; *Indian Opinion* publishes twelve chapters and eight chapters on 11 and 18 December 1909, respectively of *Hind Swarajya*; Congress Session at Lahore seeks ban on indenture system; Thomas F. Taylor; *The Fallacy of Speed* (1909) as a follow-up reading.

1910 First Gujarati edition as *Hind Swarajya* published by International Printing Press; government interpreters (Bombay High Court and Chennai Hights Court) dub the text as anti-government or seditious literature; Prohibition under the India Press Act, 1910 on 24 March; First English Edition of *Hind Swaraj* with a new foreword published by International Printing Press; Gandhi sends English edition to the secretary, Home Department; Government unmoved; prohibition under the Sea Customs Act; Gandhi sends *Indian Home Rule* to Tolstoy; Tolstoy answers on the significance of passive resistance; Gandhi establishes Tolstoy Farm near Johannesburg.

1913 Gandhi gets arrested on 6, 8, and 9 November; arrest of Kasturba.

1914 The Indians' Relief Act; Gandhi leaves South Africa forever; World War I begins (and ends in 1918); second Gujarati edition of *Hind Swaraj*

1915 Gandhi receives the "Kaisar-e-Hind" medal; becomes vice president of Gujarat Sabha; establishes "Satyagraha Ashram", Kochrab; the first Dalit family of Dudabhai, Danibehn and Laxmi join the Ashram; first Satyagraha at Viramgam, Gujarat to remove custom harassment of passengers.

1916 Speech at the opening of Benaras Hindu University (4 February); speech on "Ashram Vows" at Y.M.C.A., Madras (*Indian Review*, 16 February; vows on truth, the doctrine of ahimsa, celibacy, control of palate, non-thieving, swadeshi, fearlessness, regarding the untouchables, education through vernacular languages, hand weaving, politics.

1917 In charge of the first Gujarat Political Conference (Godhara); heads the second Gujarati Education Conference (Bharuch); establishment of Sabarmati Ashram; follows Rajkumar Shukla to Patna to find out the status of the indigo farmers; launches a successful Satyagraha campaign in Champaran; makes a statement in court about the disobedience of prohibitory orders.

1918 Delivers a speech to peasants in Nadiad, urging them to refrain from paying land revenue, and assumes the role of mediator in the conflict between the owners of mills and the workers in Ahmedabad.

1919 Commences publication of *Navajivan* (Gujarati) and *Young India* (English); Jallianwala Baug Massacre; fast in Ahmedabad for three days; Satyagraha against the Rowlatt Act; 1919: Indian English edition of *Indian Home Rule/Hind Swaraj* (Madras: Ganesh & Co); *Statement on Laws for Civil Disobedience* (7 April); renewal of proscription of *Hind Swaraj*.

1920 Gandhi becomes the president of All-India Home Rule League; All-India Satyagraha campaign begins; gives back

Kaisar-i-Hind medal; lays the foundation of Gujarat Vidyapith; commencement of non-cooperation; *"Swaraj in One Year"* (22 September, *Young India*); *"Swaraj in Nine Months"* (29 December, *Young India*).

1921 "The Secret of Swaraj" (19 January, *Young India*); *"Hind Swaraj or the Indian Home Rule"* (26 January, *Young India);* "The Conditions of Swaraj" (23 February, *Young India*); "Theft on Railways" (28 July, *Young India*); 1921 *Hind Swaraj* edition carries "Hind Swaraj or Indian Home Rule" in it (Madras: Ganesh & Company); "Tempering with Loyalty" (29 September, *Young India*); "A Puzzle and Its Solution" (15 December, *Young India*); "The Fear of Death" (13 October, *Young India*).

1922 "Independence" (5 January, *Young India*); "Shaking the Manes" (23 February, *Young India*); Trial for sedition for the authorship of three articles ("Tempering with Loyalty", "A Puzzle and Its Solution", "Shaking the Manes") in *Young India*; Great trial speech; pleads guilty; gets arrested with Shankerlal Banker and receives six years' imprisonment; transfers to Yeravada Prison; first Gujarati India Edition of *Hind Swarajya* (Ahmedabad: Navajivan); *Indian Home Rule* Edition with note by C. Rajagopalachari; *Hind Swaraj or The Indian Home Rule* by M.K. Gandhi (26 January 1921, *Young India*) added to it (Madras: Ganesan & Company); *Indian Home Rule* Edition by S Ganesan (Madras) with a nine-page introduction; Bardoli Taluka against payment of land revenue and civil disobedience.

1923: Demonstrates against the unfair rise in land revenue at Borsad; release of a facsimile version of *Hind Swarajya* in the author's original handwriting (Ahmedabad: Navajivan).

1924 "Schoolmasters and Lawyers" (17 April, *Young India*); "Untouchability and Swaraj" (12 June, *Young India*); *Sermon on the Sea* (aka *Hind Swaraj*), introduction by John Haynes Holmes and edited by Haridas T. Muzumdar (Chicago: Universal Publishing Company); starts fast against communal riots; becomes president of Congress at Belgaum Session.

1925 "Swaraj or Death" (21 May, *Young India*); "On the Verge of It" (21 May, *Young India*); "Teachers' Condition" (6 August, *Young India*).

1926 Defends *Hind Swaraj* on practicality and principles in "Letter to Labhshankar Mehta" (14 April, Sabarmati); "Sacrifice" (24 June, *Young India*); gives talks at Satyagraha Ashram in Ahmedabad about the Gita from 24 February to 26 November.

1927 *The Story* or *My Experiments with Truth* (volume one), translated by Mahadev Desai (Ahmedabad: Navajivan Press).

1928 *Satyagraha in South Africa*, translated by Valji Govindji Desai (Madras: S. Ganesan); "Speech on the Birth Centenary of Tolstoy" (10 September) links Western tradition and Indian tradition.

1929 *Poorna Swaraj* resolution at Lahore Congress; fixes 26 January as National Independence Day. Begins third all-India satyagraha campaign; *The Story* or *My Experiments with Truth* (volume two), translated by Mahadev Desai and Pyarelal Nair (Ahmedabad: Navajivan Press); "Letter to Satish Chandra Das Gupta" (Camp Hathras, 8 November), Gandhi rejects the selective choice of being violent or non-violent.

1930 Dandi March commences from Satyagraha Ashram with seventy-nine volunteers against unjust Salt Law; Gandhi gets arrested at Karadi and sent to Yeravada Central Jail; Gandhi calls Yeravada Jail as Yeravada Mandir; publishes *Mangal Prabhat*, a collection of weekly letters to Satyagraha Ashram from Yeravada Central Jail. The English edition (*From Yeravada Mandir: Ashram Observances*) published in 1932, translated by Valji Govindji Desai; they contain truth or *satya*, ahimsa or love, *brahmacharya* or chastity, control of palate or *swada*, non-stealing or *asetya*, non-possession or poverty or *aparigraha*, fearlessness or *abhay*, removal of untouchability or *ashprishtanivaran*, bread labour or *sharirshrama*, tolerance or equality of religion or *sarva dharma samantva*, humility or *namrata*, swadeshi.

1931 "Poor Man's Swaraj" (26 March, *Young India*); "Question of Safeguards" (16 April, *Young India*); writes the Gita in *Young India* on 6 August 1931; the beginning of civil disobedience.

1932 Gets arrested in Bombay and sent to Yeravada Jail; adopts the Civil Disobedience Resolution by the Congress Working Committee; establishes "Harijan Sevak Sangh".

1933 Commences the publication of *Harijan*, *Harijan Sevak* (Hindi), *Harijanbandhu* (Gujarati); dissolves Sabarmati Ashram and renames it as Harijan Ashram; gets arrested and imprisoned at Yeravada for four days; refusal to leave Yeravada village for Poona invites one year's imprisonment; commences fast and gets released; intends to start Individual Satyagraha.

1934 Establishment of All-India Village Industries Association; resigns from the Congress.

1938 First English edition of *Hind Swaraj* by Navajivan, with a preface by Mahadev Desai; *Aryan Path* special issue as "Hind

never ascending circles". Here, independence starts at the bottom, society is founded on truth and non-violence, and the pyramid structure, where the bottom supports the apex, is rejected.

1947 Barefoot march to Noakhali; indefinite hunger strike protesting the communal violence in Calcutta; visiting villages in Bihar impacted by violence; visits camps of refugees (Hindus and Sikhs from Punjab) in Delhi; unequivocal defence of *Hind Swaraj* ("Speech at the Prayer Meeting", 25 April 1947, Patna).

1948 Gandhi fasts for communal unity in Delhi (13–18 January); writes "Congress Position" (27 January), and "Draft Constitution of Congress/His Last Will and Testament" (29 January); assassinated on January 30.

PREFACE

M.K. Gandhi's (1869–1948) *Hind Swarajya/Indian Home Rule/ Hind Swaraj* (1909/1910) offers philosophy proper. Philosophy proper entails "categorical outlining" regarding rejecting prevalent conditions and offering alternative principles. Gandhi's "philosophy proper" contains the rejection principle and alternative principle. The rejection principle invites immediate attention due to the power of critique and the relevance of criticism. The power of critique also derives from the strength of the nature of substantive engagement, the severity of pursuance and passionate polemics. Due to the allurement of the power of critique and the prophetic merit of criticism, the rejection principle becomes the core component. It is declared and celebrated as a major part of the philosophical contribution. Scant attention is paid to the alternative principle. The alternative principle has a life after the rejection principle. Rejection is synonymized or construed as the only contribution by emphasizing the rejection principle. Rejection as the contribution becomes the major referential engagement. This is due to not taking the alternative principle seriously, thus converting it to a minor component.[1]

Furthermore, the minor component is reduced into utopia, which is likeable but unachievable. The rejection principle is endorsed for achieving inevitable rejection. The alternative principle is turned into rhetoric as likeable but unachievable. A careful reading of *Hind Swaraj* makes it clear that the alternative principle is not only backed by the rejection principle but also achievable by Satyagraha. In other words, Satyagraha can achieve Swaraj. Satyagraha causes or determines the alternative principle in the form of Swaraj.

The story of swaraj is embedded in the Satyagraha. *Hind Swaraj*, one of the major texts of M.K. Gandhi, was born out of thinking about Satyagraha and during the Satyagraha phase. It remains an invaluable source for understanding, forming and actualizing the dialogical self. The dialogical self does not unravel itself for constant engagement; it is also critical for the self. For Gandhi, swaraj is not mere ideas of self or scholastic consumption. It has to be *acted*. The *act* of satyagraha makes swaraj a living idea. Truth and nonviolence are the foundations of this dialogical self.

Satyagraha leads to collective formation against injustice and culminates into an interdependent political community or swaraj. The anti-binary principle (antithetical relationship between self and other) forms the collective self. The diversity in our everyday life or "lifeworld" ensures binding among heterogeneous social groups and acting upon continuous diversity. This makes other groups as necessary in our life as "own group". "Self" is abortive without "other". This helps to reject the process of otherness, in which "non-familiar" people or community is exhibited through caricaturing. The other is crucial for rejecting *othering*. Moreover, there is a possibility of regimentation of *self* and *other* or collective self; satyagraha becomes an essential component forever collective against injustice.

Based on satyagraha, swaraj cautions us against treating Gandhi as a theorist of rejection and a sublime defender of indigenism. The text proposes an interdependent political community backed by satyagraha. Twin principles are intertwined: *there cannot be swaraj (an interdependent political community) without Satyagraha. Satyagraha cannot be without an interdependent political community.*

Hind Swaraj is an essential treatise that offers an alternative, political community based on satyagraha. One of the *sui generis* aspects of *Hind Swaraj* is that its foundation is based on satyagraha. Swaraj is unthinkable without satyagraha. Satyagraha is aimless without swaraj. Satyagraha is transformation and arrival. The transformation of actual living conditions takes place by satyagraha, in which the victim and oppressor both transform. This transformation leads to swaraj.

Gandhi offers two categorical hints in this regard—*Hind Swaraj* (1910) and *Satyagraha in South Africa* (1928) are living testimonies. In *Hind Swaraj*, Gandhi suggests satyagraha as a way to achieve swaraj. Swaraj is a natural home rule. Satyagraha is a "soul-force" or "love-force". "Real home-rule is self-rule or self-control. The way to it is passive resistance: that is soul-force or love-force."[2] In *Satyagraha in South Africa*, he states that "*Hind Swaraj* was written in order to demonstrate the sublimity of satyagraha and that book is a true measure of my faith in its efficacy. I was perfectly indifferent to the numerical strength of the fighters on our side."[3]

Gandhi "spelt out a mass strategy and tactic for the realisation of Hind Swaraj in terms of disciplined action cantered around satyagraha".[4] Swaraj and satyagraha are "closely connected ideas".[5] In 1906, "the first meeting of swaraj and satyagraha occurred and long relationship began".[6] Moreover,

". . . the conviction that through a political movement, each individual might achieve liberation from fear with a new sense of self-esteem and personal strength, autonomy what is called 'empowerment'."[7] Gandhi's *Hind Swaraj* is a proclamation of ideological independence. It aimed ". . . to confront the anarchist and violence-prone Indian nationalist with an alternative to violence derived from Gandhi's earlier experiment with satyagraha. Equally important is the book's concern with the concept from which it takes its title. This is Gandhi's first extensive statement on swaraj , his idea of freedom."[8]

Satyagraha and swaraj need to be reconceptualized concerning the reading of *Hind Swaraj*. Reading and understanding satyagraha should take place with swaraj. Swaraj discourse must take note of satyagraha. In other words, reading (satyagraha and swaraj) in isolation from each other could not be more unhelpful. It makes satyagraha an action towards aimless philosophy and swaraj bereft of political action. Satyagraha aims at swaraj, and satyagraha precedes swaraj. Satyagraha is embedded in swaraj. Satyagraha achieves swaraj. As a philosophy proper, *Hind Swaraj* needs political action to actualize utopia or "de-utopize" swaraj.

The hyphenated reading of Satyagraha and swaraj is an antecedent for the de-utopization of swaraj, which is the substantive aim of *Hind Swaraj*.

Satyagraha offers a collective formation by political action against injustice based on truth and non-violence towards the arrival of swaraj, which is interdependence in collective living based on horizontal order; Gandhi does not condone *givenness* in swaraj, i.e., swaraj will be achieved *ipso facto*. He also does not condone aimlessness in Satyagraha, i.e. purposelessness as a guiding factor. "Satyagraha, as applied socio-political action, requires a comprehensive program of planning, preparation, and studied execution."[9] Thus, political action based on mutual (mental and material) transformation and the notion of suffering and sacrifice as well as aims against injustice or unjust laws, become the founding principle for swaraj as a political community. Gandhi's political community based on satyagraha not only distinguishes him from earlier notions of swaraj but also makes an inaugural new method of political action in the form of satyagraha, which distances itself from "passive resistance" and also from earlier notions available in several traditions. Gandhi's distinction from passive resistance is elaborated in the introduction; the fundamental difference is towards collective transformation by deontological means and bravery.

Gandhi coined "satyagraha" in 1906 against multiple atrocities against Indians, including denial of citizenship rights in South Africa. The Gujarati edition of 1909 retains the term. In the English edition, it is translated as passive resistance. This should not be treated as ambiguity but as an explanatory exercise for the English readers, who were almost aloof from the term.

Gandhi used satyagraha for the first time in a specific and universal sense. "[T]he word 'Satyagraha' does not seem to have been used anywhere so far. The words 'Satyagraha' (one whose rule of life is truth), 'Satyadhriti' (holding truth firmly), 'Satyanishtha' (absolute loyalty to truth), 'Satyawant' (one who has or possesses truth) and 'Satyasandha' (wedded to truth), occur often enough . . .' Satyagraha stands for a significant and new connotation altogether."[10] It is also interpreted as a weapon of moral power. "Gandhi's philosophy of life and his method of opposing evil are both called satyagraha."[11]

Satyagraha is a crucial way to resist unjust law. It can be extended to the disobedience of unfair laws. Gandhi's satyagraha offers many ways to fight against injustice and restore a higher form of justice. There are individual satyagraha and collective satyagraha. Unlike the collective formation in collective satyagraha in the form of non-cooperation or civil disobedience, individual satyagraha offers the opportunity to take a position and express dissent at the personal level.

Gandhi remains remarkably significant due to the introduction of satyagraha and its intertwining with swaraj. Satyagraha, or political action, could be construed as a "non-violent action" against state and non-state actors-led violence. Herein, transforming both participants in satyagraha and oppositional forces becomes crucial. It is against both state and non-state-led violence. Common inclusivity and anti-passivity models have become essential mechanisms.

Gandhi's swaraj as the interdependent political community has, among other things, two transversal values. Firstly, there is anti-binary (no us vs them) and anti-lexical priority (no duo of superiority and inferiority) theorization that treats the community in a non-hierarchical manner. This applies to all societies. Gandhi's criticism needs to be revised in understanding the historicity of communities. However, he becomes vital in terms of the non-lexical (non-hierarchized) conceptualization of communities. In other words, a community is not prioritized over other communities. This dilemma could be posed: Is it possible to envisage non-lexical communities (non-special communities) without resolving history? Gandhi's resolution of the historical question takes place instead in an unusual manner. His resolution of historical questions comes by way of political action, where there is an attempt to arrive at commonality. Experiments from the formation of ashrams to organizations are related examples. Gandhi hoped to resolve historical injustices by political action like satyagraha to arrive at swaraj. Secondly, there is transversal as non-territorialized theorization. His "modern civilization" critique is a non-territorial critique. In other words, it is not a nation-state-specific critique but a critique of pursuance of imperialist objectives. In this regard, Gandhi rejects binaries between countries and priorities of one or one set of countries over others. In this category of transverse, binaries are absent in acquiring domination over others.

Hind Swaraj has acquired the status of the text that offers constant opportunities for reading and interpretation. Multi-interpretative domains have paved the way for the democratization of "Gandhian studies" and critically expanded the scope for multi-layered reading. Therefore, despite some critical absence, *Hind Swaraj* has been able to invite multidimensional substantive attention. The interpretative domain has enriched the *Hind Swaraj* in and around and beyond *it*. This set of scholarship has made Gandhi and *Hind Swaraj* crucially relevant and widespread.

As a text, it has a powerful presence. "*Hind Swaraj* is the seed from which the tree of Gandhian thought has grown to its full stature. For those interested in Gandhi's thoughts in general, it is the right place to start, for it is here that he presents his basic ideas in their proper relationship to one another. And, for those who wish to study his thoughts more methodically, it remains the norm by which to assess the theoretical significance of his other writings, including the *Autobiography*. It can also save them from the danger of otherwise getting drowned in the vast sea of Gandhian anthologies."[12] It ". . . is arguably the greatest text to have emerged from the anti-colonial movement in India and perhaps the first to seriously challenge the cultural and civilizational premises of the colonizers" mentality. It is also the first text in India that falls recognizably within the broad tradition of modern political philosophy, advancing a complex cluster of theses with conceptual sensitivity, analytical precision, and sustained argument".[13] ". . . *Hind Swaraj* remained the touchstone of his beliefs and actions throughout his life, it was the fountainhead of his inspiration."[14] "The central question of *Hind Swaraj* is thus how Indians can free themselves from a position of apparent powerlessness."[15] "*Hind Swaraj* (1909) is the primary text of Gandhi's civic nationalism."[16]

Some arguments state that "[t]he language of *Hind Swaraj* is uncompromisingly moralistic".[17] "Gandhi's condemnation of machinery, and modern civilisation, in *Hind Swaraj* rests on a kind of moral fundamentalism rather than on reasoned argument."[18] The contrary argument suggests that "[t]he theme of *Hind Swaraj* was not just the moral inadequacy and extravagant pretensions of modern civilisation, but its treacherously deceptive self-destructiveness."[19]

One of the crucial debates around *Hind Swaraj* is about modernity, anti-modernity, postmodernity or alternative modernity. *Hind Swaraj* is also read in the context of modernity and subalterns.[20] According to the modernity argument, "Gandhi's *Hind Swaraj* is not a rejection of the liberative contribution of modernity: civil liberties, religious tolerance, equality, poverty alleviation. Rather his effort can be interpreted as an attempt to integrate these positive elements with a liberating re-interpretation of tradition, even as some see him as radical and others as reactionary. With his critique from within the tradition, Gandhi becomes the great synthesiser of contraries if not of contradictions, within and across traditions."[21]

In another reading, *Hind Swaraj* is construed as an "anti-modernist tract".[22] It must be contextualized.

Gandhi was convinced that India in 1909 stood at the crossroads that Europe found itself in the Early Modern period. The harsh words that Gandhi reserves for Western modernity were expressive of the fear that India would go down the lamentable path of some of the worst aspects of *politics and political economy* that have characterised the passage in Europe from Early to Late Modernity. And the entire book tries to provide a genealogical and diagnostic account of the *cognitive and cultural sources and effects* of those aspects of politics and the political economy of Europe's past and present that have never had any place in Indian society, however defective Indian society may otherwise be, and which would do no favours to India were India to embrace them, an embrace that seemed to him very much in the offing, given the fact that India was not merely being subjected to imperial subjugation but to a determined effort to enslave it in cognitive and cultural terms."[23]

Hind Swaraj also invites attention as a text of postmodernity. "As early as 1909, in his seminal essay, *Hind Swaraj*, Gandhi formulated the term "modern civilization" and found it wanting. In doing so he flew in the face of prevailing world opinion."[24] Gandhian alternatives have become significant in modernization.[25] "Gandhi sought to forge an alternative modernity."[26]

Civilizational discourse is another critical component. *Hind Swaraj* is termed a performative text and ontological drama. It "can actually be read as an attempt to "awaken the dead" and to put together what has been smashed—not merely by British colonialism, as Gandhi repeatedly reminds us, but by modern civilization. It is therefore dramatic, excessive and often deliberately provocative . . . a performative text".[27] Moreover, "[i]n this ontological drama, empirical details do not really matter, for it was the "existential truth" of the modern condition that he was bringing out."[28] *Hind Swaraj*

"... depicts a "clash of civilizations". It is a clash between values, and since it deals with normative systems, it maps the political terrain differently; Gandhi is not so much interested in expostulating upon events happening in the outer world, but in reading its meanings for the normative constitution of individual and collective psyche, its downfall and its rejuvenation."[29]

However, another argument suggests that:

Hind Swaraj is less a manifesto, a credo, or a diatribe against Western civilization. It is, instead, a text that tussles with a late Victorian inheritance of the crisis within liberalism in Europe; a growing disaffection with its imperial form in India; and disquiet with the forms of popular politics that challenged the imperial formation in India. In many senses, Gandhi embodied Nordau's "new conservative" mentioned earlier, in his search for the proper form of politics and self-making, for which there was no immediate resolution."[30]

Speed is also a critical component in studying *Hind Swaraj*. "While for Gandhi, speedings are histories interrupting the formation of the critical nation and apocalypses are autolyses, ends of histories, which are always survived by the slow, from which progenies would arise again."[31] The structuring force is another crucial dimension to understanding *Hind Swaraj*. "Beneath the hyperbolic polarization of sovereign and subject, east and west, in *Hind Swaraj*, both west and east are subjugated by a subsuming entity, a structuring force that determines the "condition" of England and through it of India."[32] The text is a castigation of the evils of Western imperialism. "Thoreau and Tolstoy had said the same thing, and their influence is particularly strong in Gandhi's *Hind Swaraj* (Indian Home Rule), a severe castigation of the evils of Western imperialism which enslaved colonial peoples and brought material prosperity to the governing nations."[33]

The political theory of *Hind Swaraj* is a theory of the peasant community.[34] The text also interprets passive revolution, including India and self-rule at individual and institutional levels. Regarding the passive revolution, "[b]eginning its journey from the utopianism of *Hind Swaraj*, and yet picking up on the way the ideological baggage of a nationalist politics, Gandhism succeeded in opening up the historical possibility by which the largest popular element of the nation—the peasantry—could be appropriated within the evolving political forms of the new Indian state."[35] Concerning the inclusivity,

> The very name of this text, "*Hind Swaraj*", which made use of what was essentially an Urdu name for India ("Hind", rather than "Bharat"), is one indication of Gandhi's care to ensure that his "India" should not signify any association with a single tradition. Moreover, he made it clear that the Indian nation was not linked to any single religion . . .[36]

Moreover, the arguments in *Hind Swaraj* were meant for India in place of Indians in South Africa. "At one level, swaraj or self-rule must mean an individual's rule over himself or herself. At the political level, it means home rule or self-government. But if it is to satisfy, self-government must be grounded on the control that leaders and citizens exercise over themselves."[37]

This book uses "the formative principle" of the *Hind Swaraj* to understand both the rejection and alternative principles it offers. For this reason, locating the text in 1910 becomes significant. Besides restoring the Promethean of the 1910 English edition, it also reminds us of the unfulfilled promises of rejections and unfulfilled principles of an alternative world. In the formative principle, the text's ontological concern constantly reminds us of the immediate and universal purpose while going beyond the constraints of time and the limits of space. Reading the 1910 edition also reinforces the obligation of reminding people of unfilled actions towards rejection and unfulfilled actions towards the alternative.

This book contains an introduction and *Hind Swaraj*. *Hind Swaraj's* 1910 (International Printing Press, Phoenix, Natal) edition is reproduced here. In his remarkable edited edition *of Hind Swaraj and other writings*, Anthony Parel used the 1910 edition of the *Hind Swaraj*.[38] Suresh Sharma and Tridip Suhrud's M.K. Gandhi's *Hind Swaraj* also contains the 1910 edition. The editors translated *Hind Swaraj* from Gujarati into Hindi for this edition.[39] S. R. Mehrotra's *Indian Home Rule* [Hind Swaraj],[40] and Usha Thakkar and Gita Dharampal's *Hind Swaraj: Mohandas Karamchand Gandhi* also used the 1910 English edition.[41]

In the annotations, the diversion from the 1939 revised new edition (Navajivan Press, Ahmedabad) is mentioned, related to the punctuation and restructuring of sentences. According to Mahadev Desai, for the 1939 revised new edition, "[t]he proof copy of this edition has been revised by numerous friends to whom I am deeply indebted."[42] The revised new edition of 1939 will be denoted as RNE. In a few places, Gujarati equivalent words from the 1909 edition (11 and 18 December 1909, *Indian Opinion*) are mentioned in the endnotes. *CWMG* stands for *Collected Works of Mahatma Gandhi* (The Publications Division, Ministry of Information and Broadcasting, Government of India).

Concerning translation and authenticity of meaning, the 1910 English edition of the *Hind Swaraj* must be considered a progressive translation of 1909's Gujarati *Hind Swarajya,* published in two instalments in *Indian Opinion,* later in the full-length book in 1910. Progressive translation entails re-clarification for immediate concepts or categories or unambiguous ideas by revising and dropping a few words and sentences here and there. In the context of *Autobiography,* Gopalkrishna Gandhi offers a significant suggestion that could also be helpful in reading and re-reading Gandhi's *Hind Swaraj.* According to him, "[v]ariations in a translation are not "defects", as in this particular work [*Autobiography*], the stamp of the author's approval is implicit, the variations have to be taken as "revisions" that "re-phrase" the original for one or more reason, being as much by the author as by the translator."[43] For Tridip Suhrud, "[t]hus, in many of its central concerns, *Hind Swaraj* is a bilingual text . . . conceived simultaneously in two linguistic frames and rendered in two languages. It needs to be read in both languages as two original texts . . . not one as original and the other as a derivative translation."[44]

Paraphrasing the argument for the *Hind Swaraj* (English, 1910), it might be stated that variations between Gujarati and English editions of the *Hind Swaraj* should not be considered a defect. In the case of *Hind Swaraj,* Gandhi is the author and translator. Thus, the English version should be treated as revisions as rephrasing the original for various reasons. Thus, the annotations will have very limited mandates concerning the meaning in both languages. Some words from the original will be given in the case to enhance the meaning of the present text. Therefore, only in a few cases will omissions from the Gujarati text be mentioned.

For the annotations, the following style is used: the first Gujarati edition of the Hind Swaraj (as published in Indian Opinion) as 1909-GE; the 1939 revised new English edition as RNE; the first Hindi Edition of *Hind Swaraj* of 1959 *as* 1959-HE.

By emphasizing the "formative principle", this edition endeavours to make swaraj by way of satyagraha the central tenet of the reading, *Hind Swaraj*. In both cases, rejection and alternative principles, there is a significance of inseparability between satyagraha and swaraj. The 1910 edition reminds us of the Promethean value of satyagraha and swaraj and, after that, the universalization of the alternative principle. In a nutshell, reading the 1910 English edition, among other things, becomes crucial on four grounds:

1. It offers Gandhi's original foreword, essential for considering epistemic diversity.
2. It highlights and reminds us of the birth of swaraj against the backdrop of satyagraha.
3. Satyagraha must be treated as swaraj's alter ego.
4. Satyagraha is not a forgotten principle or action for a political community theorised on or based on swaraj.

In other words, swaraj, through satyagraha, should give place to hyphenated reading and understanding of satyagraha and *Hind Swaraj*. Satyagraha and swaraj intertwine and give birth to Gandhian heterodoxy. Gandhi's heterodoxy makes the "alternative possible" through the principle of reconciliation and antagonism. The principle of reconciliation aims at reconciliation among beings. The other precedes the self. This means the self cannot annihilate others. In fact, there is no self sans others. This has invited wider attention. This missing component is the principle of antagonism.

The principle of antagonism against unjust structures through satyagraha gives birth to people as sovereigns who constantly remind the political community about its ontological foundations. Herein, people are reminded about people as the foundation of a political community based on truth and non-violence. Truth helps reject the sermonization of teleological givenness, which is perceiving events uncritically. Non-violence makes the "body" equal in worth but not more than others.

INTRODUCTION

Reading the *Hind Swaraj* begets synthesization between satyagraha and swaraj. In his book *Satyagraha in South Africa* (1928), Gandhi mentions the eight years (1906–14) of satyagraha in South Africa. "Thus the great Satyagraha struggle closed after eight years, and it appeared that the Indians in South Africa were now at peace."[1] Gandhi stated in 1910 that his "ideas . . . about Satyagraha had now matured and I had realized its universality as well as its excellence. I was therefore perfectly at ease. *Hind Swaraj* was written in order to demonstrate the sublimity of Satyagraha and that book is a true measure of my faith in its efficacy."[2] The number count remained insignificant. "I was perfectly indifferent to the numerical strength of the fighters on our side."[3]

Hind Swaraj was an outcome during the period of satyagraha in Africa. The years 1906–09 (the year of writing of *Hind Swaraj*) are crucial in which Gandhi himself saw the transition from "the earnest petitioner" to "the unwilling petitioner". "The renunciation of London" becomes definite in *Hind Swaraj*.[4] Underneath these significant changes, the critical responsible factors were his encounter with the political process of England, exposure and realization of the universal civilizational mission on racial fault lines and economic plundering by British Imperialism, his appreciation and criticism of women passive resisters of London on violence; rejection of a motley group located in London whom Gandhi called the "Indian school of violence"[5] or people associated with India House;[6] significant diversion on reading an understanding of Indian religious texts from the Indian school of violence;[7] making civilizational discourse important; avoiding religious binaries in analysis.[8]

Gandhi's rejection principle in the *Hind Swaraj* is profound. His "alternative principle" was also based on the realization of the limits of liberalism of the empire,[9] both in South Africa and India, where laws catapulted the sovereignty of *res publica* supreme in place of people as sovereign.

Gandhi's presence and activism became necessary due to imperialist development, which connected England, South Africa and India.

The British acquired South Africa from the Dutch because it was a station on the way to India. The descendants of the Dutch, the Boer farmers, trekked inland to remain free of British rule (and may well have remained so, had not gold been discovered in their land), while the British settled along the coasts of the Cape Colony and Natal. In Natal they found a land rich in agricultural and mineral resources but lacking in labor. The native blacks, commonly called Kaffirs, were unwilling to be converted into settled laborers on the estates and in the mines. Slavery having been abolished throughout the Empire as of 1834, the Natal settlers appealed to India for workers under an indenture system so restrictive as to be labelled "a new form of slavery".[10]

Indians were allowed 'lawfully' to come to South Africa as 'precarious beings' in the form of indentured labourers and traders and service providers. This is the case when 'law' becomes the legitimacy of 'lawlessness' or law without justice for perpetuating a slew of laws for making Indians /Asians 'permanent outsiders'.

British Secretary of State for the Colonies, the Natal Collie Law, Law 14 of 1859, permitted the colony to admit the Indian migrants as indentured labourers. By 1876, Indians were made to understand that they had no permanent right to residence. Transvaal passed *Law 3 of 1885* against Asians concerning not allowing burgher and property rights and providing for inscribing in a register. 1888 witnessed carrying pass provisions for Indians who were no longer indentured labourers. *The Orange Free State Act 29* was against the influx of Asiatics. In 1891, business and framing were prohibited. *Act 25 of 1891* withdrew the full citizenship rights of indentured labourers. *The Franchise Act of 1894* enabled Natal to disenfranchise Indians. *Act 17 of 1895* imposed a £3 tax on ex-indentured labourers who were not available for re-indenture or unwilling to return to India. This was also extended to boys (sixteen years and above) and girls (twelve years and above) in 1901. The punishment was imprisonment or deportation—*the Franchise Act No. 8 of 1896* disenfranchised Indians in Natal. *The Dealers Licenses Act, No. 18* sanctioned the right to issue and not issue licenses in Natal. Transvaal, through *the Law of 1897*, prohibited marriage between whites and coloured people. The *Regulation for Towns in South Africa Republic (Transvaal)* prohibited persons of colour from walking on pavements. *The Immigration Restricted Act of 1905* restricted immigration from India to Natal and introduced a special permit system for Indians to enter Transvaal. *The Immigration Act of 1906* introduced a literacy requirement for Indians to enter the cape colony. The most brutal was *The Asiatic Law Amendment Ordinance 29 of 1906 (Transvaal)*, which proposed compulsory registration, identification by fingerprints and mandatorily carrying certificates all the time and its production on demand by police. All Indians were subjected to it. *The Asiatic Law Amendment Act, 2/1907* asked all male Asians to register, always provide fingerprints and carry passes. Even a workman was defined as white in *The Workmen's Compensation Act, 36/1907* in Transvaal, followed by an education test, i.e., *Education Act, No 25 of 1907, Transvaal*. In 1908, *The Immortality Amendment Ordinance 16/1908)* allowed persons of colour to live in townships as domestic workers in Transvaal. *The Immigration Regulation Act, no 22 of 1913,* laid down the provision for exclusion from the country on the grounds of non-literacy in European languages and economic conditions. Finally, *the Indian Relief Act of 1914* was passed due to satyagraha in South Africa, based on the findings of the Solomon Commission.[11] The act was a significant achievement, if not very comprehensive.

There were some significant moments for Gandhi upon his arrival in South Africa (Durban) in 1893—his arrival as a lawyer for Dada Abdulla; being removed from the first-class compartment at Pietermaritzburg (Natal) on way to Pretoria (Transvaal); being beaten during a stagecoach journey from Charlestown to Johannesburg; encountering the second-hand experience in the form of knowing that Indians paid £3 as a poll tax in Transvaal and subsequent encounters with laws mentioned above; despite a lawful authorization letter to walk on a public street and also beyond a 9 p.m. restriction, being assaulted near the house of President Kruger; enrolling himself as a lawyer in the Supreme Court of Natal; establishment of the Natal Indian Congress (NIC) (1894); facing anger of whites over the Green Pamphlets while returning to South Africa from India in 1896; double dilemma (because of his sympathy for the Boers, but his receiving of rights as a British subject, which led to the formation of the Ambulance Corps during the Second Anglo-Boer War [1899–1901]); after his disillusionment with Joseph Chamberlain (the British Secretary of State for the Colonies), enrolment as a lawyer in Transvaal; formation of Indian Ambulance Crops during Zulu Rebellion; formation of the British Indian Association (1903) and starting of *Indian Opinion*; reading *Unto This Last* by John Ruskin; establishment of the Phoenix settlement in Durban; taking the vow of celibacy (1906); the beginning of satyagraha (1906) against unjust laws; refusal of Indians to register and beginning of arrests in 1907–08; usage of the term the Black Act and beginning of satyagraha against it; his arrest in 1908; 'bonfire' of registration certificates; two-month sentence in 1908; three-month sentence in 1909; acceptance of the proposal for voluntary registration; attack on Gandhi for accepting this proposal; non-repeal of the Black Act; establishment of Tolstoy Farm in 1910; Gokhale's visit to South Africa 1912; defiance of the Immigrations Act of 1913; arrest of Gandhi; release of Gandhi and the passing of the Indian Relief Act.

Chapter Twelve (Advent of Satyagraha) and Thirteen (Satyagraha vs Passive Resistance) of *Satyagraha in South Africa* are crucial to understanding satyagraha's significance. A mass meeting of Indians took place. The meeting of Indians at Johannesburg against the Transvaal Asiatic Law Amendment Ordinance on 11 September 1906 was an important landmark. Addressing this meeting, Gandhi said, "[t]he old Empire Theatre was packed from floor to ceiling. I could read in every face the expectation of something strange to be done or to happen . . .

The most important among the resolutions passed by the meeting was the famous Fourth Resolution, by which the Indians solemnly determined not to submit to the Ordinance in the event of its becoming law in the teeth of their opposition and to suffer all the penalties attaching to such non-submission."[12] This resolution was explained in multiple languages. By way of god's reference, he added, "[a] man who makes an ordinary resolution is not ashamed of himself when he deviates from it, but a man who violates an oath administered to him is not only ashamed of himself, but is also looked upon by society as a sinner."[13]

This was stated "that . . . if a majority of the Indians pledge themselves to resistance and if all who take the pledge prove true to themselves, the Ordinance may not be passed and, if passed, may be soon repealed. It may be that we may not be called upon to suffer at all . . . Imagine that all of us present here numbering 3,000 at the most pledge ourselves. Imagine again that the remaining 10,000 Indians take no such pledge. We will only provoke ridicule in the beginning . . . "[14] In the backdrop of the government's exception to women in the Ordinance, he stated, "[i]t is difficult to say whether the exemption of women was the first fruit of the community's agitation, or whether the Government as an afterthought made a concession to practical considerations . . . Government claimed that it had decided to exempt women independently of the Indian agitation. Be that as it might, the community established to their own satisfaction a cause-and-effect relation between the agitation and the exemption and their fighting spirit rose accordingly. None of us knew what name to give to our movement. I then used the term 'passive resistance' in describing it."[15]

Due to confusion over the term passive resistance, another term was envisaged. For this, "[a] small prize was therefore announced in *Indian Opinion* to be awarded to the reader who invented the best designation for our struggle . . . Shri Maganlal Gandhi was one of the competitors and he suggested the word 'Sadagraha,' meaning 'firmness in a good cause'. I liked the word, but it did not fully . . . represent the whole idea therefore corrected it to 'Satyagraha'. Truth (Satya) implies love, and firmness (agraha) engenders and therefore serves as a synonym for force. I thus began to call the Indian movement 'Satyagraha', that is to say, the Force which is born of Truth and Love or non-violence, and gave up the use of the phrase 'passive resistance', in connection with it, so much so that even in English writing we often avoided it and used instead the word 'Satyagraha' itself or some other equivalent English phrase."[16]

For Gandhi, the difference between satyagraha and passive resistance is fundamental. Against the formulation of the general belief of passive resistance as a 'weapon of the weak', he defined his notion of passive resistance as a soul force that is satyagraha.

Satyagraha is soul force pure and simple, and whenever and to whatever extent there is room for the use of arms or physical force or brute force, there and to that extent is there so much less possibility for soul force. . . . Again, while there is no scope for love in passive resistance, on the other hand not only has hatred no place in Satyagraha but is a positive breach of its ruling principle. While in passive resistance there is a scope for the use of arms when a suitable occasion arrives, in Satyagraha physical force is forbidden even in the most favourable circumstances. Passive resistance is often look[ed] upon as a preparation for use of force while Satyagraha can never be utilized as such. Passive resistance may be offered side by side with the use of arms. Satyagraha and brute force, being each a negation of the other, can never go together. Satyagraha may be offered to one's nearest and dearest; passive resistance can never be offered to them unless of course they have ceased to be dear and become an object of hatred to us. In passive resistance there is always present an idea of harassing the other party and there is a simultaneous readiness to undergo any hardships entailed upon us by such activity, while in Satyagraha there is not the remotest idea of injuring the opponent. Satyagraha postulates the conquest of the adversary by suffering in one's own person.[17]

In the *Autobiography*, chapter twenty-six is titled "The Birth of Satyagraha".

Gandhi left with Haji Habib on deputation for the Indian cause for England from South Africa on 21 June 1909, and reached London on 10 July 1909. They left England on 13 November 1909 and reached South Africa on 30 November 1909. This was the crucial period for engaging with Tolstoy and writing a letter to Polak in 1909. In a "Letter to Tolstoy", in addition to appraising the value of his own practice of satyagraha, Gandhi also sought permission to publish *A Letter to a Hindoo* in English and Gujarati. The *Letter* "was in reply to a "Letter to Tolstoy" by the editors of an underground journal named *Free Hindustan,* issued from Vancouver. Its chief editor was Tarak Nath Das. Tolstoy's letter was published in *Indian Opinion,* 25-12-1909 and 1-1-1910, with a preface by Gandhiji. A Gujarati translation by him was also published, first in *Indian Opinion,* later, in the form of a book."[18] Gandhi wrote to Tolstoy that "[i]t is the intention of my friend,[19] at his own expense, to have 20,000 copies printed and distributed and to have it translated also."[20] Tolstoy gave his consent in a letter dated 7 October 1909.[21] "Das and *Free Hindusthan* are important in tracing the historical link between Gandhi and Tolstoy, and the development of some of the arguments in *Hind Swaraj* . . . A typescript of this work was circulating in Indian revolutionary circles in Paris in 1909, and it fell into Gandhi's hands while he was still in London, sent to him from Paris by his friend Dr Pranjivan Mehta . . . The translation and the editing took place on board the Kildonan Castle, during the same week that he wrote *Hind Swaraj*."[22]

Gandhi wrote a letter to Henry Polak ("Letter to H.S. Polak", 14 October 1909, London). This encapsulates the certain outline of *Hind Swaraj*. This letter examines the anatomy of "modern civilization" with the aim of restoring people's autonomy. In this letter, Gandhi asserts his stance against territoriality and racial arguments, while also drawing a distinction between Western/ European and modern civilization. People's connection in the pre-imperialist era is an important aspect. Modern civilization is an extension of control. He also provides a critique of urbanism. He does not replicate the political system, but instead seeks an alternative. An alternative can serve as a meeting point for East and West. Individual concerns alone cannot drive the changes. He highlights the conflict between materiality and morality. In the medical sciences, there is a critique of opacity. Hospitals face criticism for their lack of morality in treating patients. Many times, unlearning becomes an essential requirement. Machine-made clothing is to be rejected. In this endeavour, assistance from England is critical. People's salvation is linked to the aphorism described below in the letter:

1. There is no impassable barrier between East and West.
2. There is no such thing as Western or European civilization, but there is a modern civilization, which is purely material.

3. The people of Europe, before they were touched by modern civilization, had much in common with the people of the East; anyhow, the people of India and, even today, Europeans who are not touched by modern civilization are far better able to mix with the Indians than the offspring of that civilization.

4. It is not the British people who are ruling India, but it is modern civilization, through its railways, telegraphs, telephones and almost every invention which has been claimed to be a triumph of civilization.

5. Bombay, Calcutta and the other chief cities of India are the real plague spots.

6. If British rule were replaced tomorrow by Indian rule based on modern methods, India would be no better, except that she would be able then to retain some of the money that is drained away to England; but then, Indians would only become a second or fifth edition of Europe or America.

7. East and West can only and really meet when the West has thrown overboard modern civilization, almost in its entirety. They can also seemingly meet when East has adopted modern civilization. But that meeting would be an armed truce, even as it is between, say, Germany and England, both of which nations are living in the Hall of Death in order to avoid being devoured, the one by the other.

8. It is simply impertinence for any man or any body of men to begin or contemplate reform of the whole world. To attempt to do so by means of highly artificial and speedy locomotion is to attempt the impossible.

9. Increase of material comforts, it may be generally laid down, does not in any way whatsoever conduce to moral growth.

10. Medical science is the concentrated essence of Black Magic. Quackery is infinitely preferable to what passes for high medical skill.

11. Hospitals are the instruments that the Devil has been using for his own purpose, in order to keep his hold on his kingdom. They perpetuate vice, misery and degradation and real slavery.

12. I was entirely off the track when I considered that I should receive a medical training. It would be sinful for me in any way whatsoever to take part in the abominations that go on in the hospitals.

    If there were no hospitals for venereal diseases, or even for consumptives, we should have less consumption, and less sexual vice amongst us.

13. India's salvation consists in unlearning what she has learnt during the past fifty years. The railways, telegraphs, hospitals, lawyers, doctors and such like have all to go, and the so-called upper classes have to learn to live conscientiously and religiously and deliberately the simple peasant life, knowing it to be a life-giving true happiness.

14. Indians should wear no machine-made clothing, whether it comes out of European mills or Indian mills.

15. England can help India to do this, and then she will have justified her hold of India. There seem to be many in England today who think likewise.

16. There was true wisdom in the sages of old having so regulated society as to limit the material condition of the people: the rude plough of perhaps five thousand years ago is the plough of the husbandman today. Therein lies salvation. People live long, under such conditions, in comparative peace much greater than Europe has enjoyed after having taken up modem activity, and I feel that every enlightened man, certainly every Englishman, may, if he chooses, learn this truth and act according to it.[23]

A Letter to a Hindoo and *Hind Swaraj* were worked upon together. "Once on board the S.S. Kildonan Castle on 13 November 1909, on his voyage back to South Africa, Gandhi busied himself for the first seven days with the translation of 'Letter to a Hindoo' into Gujarati and writing two 'prefaces' to it—the first in Gujarati and the second in English, both published in *Indian Opinion* on 25 December 1909. This may account for the excited and almost exalted *Hind Swarajya* during the subsequent three days, 20 to 22 November 1909."[24] According to D.G. Tendulkar, Gandhi wrote his 30,000-word famous book *Hind Swaraj* while working ". . . day and night over the manuscript from November 13 to November 22, and wrote in on the steamer's stationery, in all 271 pages, about fifty pages he wrote with the left hand because his right hand was exhausted".[25] Gandhi did not make any changes or corrections after 22 November 1910.[26] According to Suresh Sharma and Tridip Suhrud, ". . . .Gandhi wrote with the left hand thirty-eight full pages and 62 lines spread over nine pages."[27] Prabhudas Gandhi offers an important insight concerning "how Hind Swaraj was written". "Turning over the pages of the manuscript, one realizes Gandhiji's genius as a writer. In the 275 hand-written pages, only three lines have been scratched out. A few words here and there have been changed. When Gandhiji tired of writing with his right hand, he wrote with his left. "There are 40 pages, including a whole chapter at the end of the book, which he wrote with his left hand."[28]

Indian Opinion published twelve and eight chapters on 11 and 18 December 1909 respectively. The first Gujarati edition book was published in January 1910 by International Printing Press (Phoenix, South Africa), soon to be followed by proscription by the Government of Bombay on 24 March 1910. Gandhi himself translated the text from Gujarati to English and published it in March 1910 through the same press. The second Gujarati edition was published in May 1914. This was followed by the publication of the first English edition in India by Ganesh and Company, Madras. In 1924, H.T. Mazumdar edited the American edition *of Sermon on the Sea,* which was published in the USA by Universal Publishing Company, Chicago. The first English edition (as claimed) contains a preface by Mahadev Desai and a revised English edition, both by Navajivan, published in 1938 and 1939. Amrutlal Thakoredas Nanavati translated and published *Hind Swaraj* in 1959 in Hindi by Navajivan, which also contained the preface of Kaka Kalelkar (1885–1991).[29]

Reading of Hind Swaraj

'Hind Swaraj proscribed.'

This was one of the news items published in *Indian Opinion* on 19 March 1910 in Gujarati under the heading of Johannesburg. According to the report, this step was expected. Some of the arguments in the book tend to be against British rule. Gandhi was involved in the Transvaal agitation for the rights of Indians. The agitation Gandhi led in Transvaal/South Africa and authorship of the *Hind Swaraj* were considered connected. *Satyagrahi* in Transvaal was considered satyagrahi in other circumstances. The impact of the *Hind Swaraj* on the Transvaal agitation could strengthen or weaken the cause. The Transvaal campaign was crucial for the swaraj in India.[30] Right after this, Gandhi wrote the *Preface to Indian Home Rule,* a translation of the Gujarati work *Hind Swarajya,* on 20 March 1910.[31]

In the preface, he started discussing the translation with a European friend and several English friends. "A European friend, with whom I discussed the contents, wanted to see a translation of it and, during our spare moments, I hurriedly dictated and he took it down. It is not a literal translation but it is a faithful rendering of the original."[32] This European friend of Gandhi was Hermann Kallenbach.[33] Hereafter, the story went in two directions regarding satyagraha. Although both were intertwined, their nature differed significantly. The first small house, The Kraal (now known as Satyagraha House), was built in 1907 on the outskirts of Johannesburg, South Africa. Kallenbach designed the house. Gandhi and Kallenbach stayed in the house from 1908 to 1909 before moving to the Tolstoy Farm, which became the new site for passive resistance. This was the place where satyagraha was conceptualized.[34] This was the period when *Hind Swaraj* was written.

Gandhi sent *Hind Swaraj* to Tolstoy for his comments and criticisms ("Letter to Leo Tolstoy", 4 April 1910).[35] Upon receiving the book *Indian Home Rule/Hind Swaraj*, Tolstoy sent an appreciation letter to Gandhi ("Tolstoy's Letter to Gandhiji", 8 May 1910). Tolstoy was also drawn to "passive resistance" in *Hind Swaraj*. "I read your book with great interest because I think that the question you treat in it—the passive resistance—is a question of great importance not only for India but for the whole humanity."[36]

In the second, he also shared the draft with "[s]everal English friends . . . [to] . . . read it, and . . . opinions were being invited as to the advisability of publishing the work . . . "[37] W. J. Wybergh, a member of the Legislative Assembly, Transvaal, offered a nuanced criticism of *Hind Swaraj*. On 2 May 1910, he wrote a letter to Gandhi on the draft, which was published in *Indian Opinion* on

21 May 1910.[38] He expressed his inability to give full comment due to a lack of coherence in Gandhi's argument. However, he found that Gandhi's position varied with common opinion. For example, despite avoiding a concrete charge of disloyalty, the book is highly dangerous. "Granting that you do not intend to be disloyal, yet I am sure that the average plain ignorant man without intellectual subtlety would suppose that you were preaching against British rule in India, for you attack everything which the plain man would identify with this rule."[39]

For him, the underlying principle of the book is wrong. Despite many defects in European civilization, it cannot be the kingdom of Satan. He highlights the significance of civilization for India. In addition to Indian questions, he focuses on passive resistance and non-resistance. Firstly, Gandhi is "confusing between 'passive resistance' and 'non-resistance'".[40] He accuses Gandhi of shifting the battle from physical force to the mental plane and denies the linkages between soul force/passive resistance and love or spirituality. "What you call 'soul-force' and 'passive resistance' have nothing to do with love or spirituality in themselves. In advocating these things instead of physical force, you are only transferring the battle and the violence from the physical to the mental plane. Your weapons are mental and psychic, not physical, but also not spiritual."[41] "I regard all possible means of *intellectual persuasion and argument* as right and necessary, I think that the use of what you call "soul-force" for concrete ends as dangerous in the extreme . . . "[42] He extends his support to governments, laws, the police and physical force as natural stages of development.

Wybergh cautions against the politicization of passive resistance and linking with martyrs, complaining about prison hardship and gaining political capital through advertisement in the Press or sending deputations to England and India. "If it is really a matter of religion, then I think that the truest heroism is not concerned in this exceedingly active 'passive resistance' but that it consists in suffering as *private individuals* and saying nothing about it."[43] He does not accord the superiority of passive resisters to other categories. "I admire heroism displayed in a political cause, and the very real heroism of many 'passive resisters', I must say that it seems in no way superior to the more active forms displayed by soldiers or rioters or revolutionaries . . . The physical sufferings of soldiers at any rate have vastly exceeded those of 'passive resisters'"[44]. "To undermine them without being ready to substitute something else a little better but still of the same character is simply to destroy the possibility of all advance. Therefore, to my mind, such preaching is far more injurious than mere disloyalty, which after all only proposes to substitute another Government."[45]

Gandhi's "Letter to W. J. Wybergh", dated 10 May 1910 was also published in the *Indian Opinion* on 21 May 1910.[46] He makes the distinction between Christianity and modern civilization. Gandhi rejects the division between religion and politics and seeks to rejoin by passive resisters in the light of ethical principles. He reasserts the contribution of "passive resister". "If you say that physical sufferings of soldiers have vastly exceeded those of the Transvaal passive resisters, I agree with you entirely; but the sufferings of world-known passive resisters who deliberately walked into funeral pyres or into boiling cauldrons were incomparably greater than those of any soldier it is possible to name."[47] Against accusing Tolstoy of being an anarchist, Gandhi defends him by obeying the principle of conscience. According to Gandhi, for Tolstoy, ". . . there is no government that can control him without his sanction. Such a man is superior to all government."[48]

Wybergh's rejection of the text for being dangerous and allusion to satyagraha with great scepticism was matching with the Government of British India. "Our Publications" in *Indian Opinion* (7 May 1910) mentioned the notification of the Bombay Government Gazette issued on 24 March 1910, forfeiting *Hind Swarajya, Universal Dawn* (Gujarati rendering of Ruskin's *Unto this Last*), *Mustafa Kamel Pasha's Speech* (Gujarati translation of his speech given before his death in Cairo) and *Defence of Socrates or The Story of a True Warrior* (Gujarati translation of Plato's work). All were published by the International Printing Press. They were forfeited to His Majesty due to their containing "matter declared to be seditious".[49] Plato's translation found a special mention herein. It was ". . . printed in order to illustrate the virtue and true nature of passive resistance".[50] All of these were written to make such ideas easily understandable, even to children. It further stated that "uncompromising advocates of passive resistance" could not be deterred by the repression. "Passive resistance" was also suggested as an effective way to negate the violence. The negation of violence could not be achieved by repression.[51]

On several occasions, Gandhi read *Hind Swaraj* in association with satyagraha.

Satyagraha Sabha issued the "Statement on Laws for Civil Disobedience" on 7 April 1919 (undersigned by M.K. Gandhi, president, Satyagraha Sabha; D.D. Sathye, Umar Sobani and Shankarlal Ghelabhai secretaries; *Bombay Chronicle*). "The Committee contemplated by the Satyagraha Pledge has advised that for the time being laws regarding prohibited literature and registration of newspapers may be civilly disobeyed" (*Bombay*

Chronicle, 8 April 1919).[52] Prohibited literature, including *Hind Swarajya,* was selected for dissemination. "Regarding prohibited literature, to select such books and pamphlets as are not inconsistent with satyagraha, and which are, therefore, of a clean type and which do not, either directly or indirectly, approve of or encourage violence."[53] The process of "how to commit civil disobedience" is outlined in the context of prohibited literature. A satyagrahi should have proscribed literature for distribution while mentioning their names and addresses in case of easy traceability by the government for prosecution. Small groups can be formed for reading such literature. Along with civil breach of laws, the aim should also be to provide high moral value. In the case of confiscation of literature, since the government is expected to confiscate the proscribed literature, satyagrahis must not only be financially independent but also make copies of prohibited literature themselves or seek assistance from friends. "When whole copies are exhausted by dissemination or confiscation, satyagrahis may continue civil disobedience by writing out and distributing extracts from accessible books."[54]

In his "Letter to Labhshankar Mehta" (Sabarmati, 14 April 1926), Gandhi defended *Hind Swaraj* on the question of practicality and principles propounded in it. "I do not think that it is right to say that the principles propounded in *Hind Swaraj* are not workable just because I cannot practice them perfectly."[55] On the question of implementation per se, he made a distinction between a resolve and a vow. He preferred the latter. "Where distinction is made between making a resolve and taking a vow, only taking a vow is worthwhile. A resolve which can be broken cannot be regarded as a resolve. It has no value at all."[56]

In 1929, Gandhi called proscription, including *Hind Swaraj,* without trial or examination without the author, a daylight robbery.[57] However, it helped the cause of civil disobedience. "The Government are by such acts providing us with easy methods of civil disobedience should it be necessary for us next year to undertake it on a large scale" (*Young India,* 4 April 1929).[58]

In the backdrop of rejecting the nature of reading of *Hind Swaraj* by Lord Ronaldshay (Governor of Bengal, 1917–22) and non-co-operationalism by Colonel Wedgwood (British Labour Leader; as a member of parliament, he visited India in 1920 and attended the Congress Session at Nagpur), he defended the book for the reader. "The swaraj that I dream of will be a possibility only when the nation is free to make its choice both good and evil."[59] "The gospel of non-co-operation addresses itself to the task of making the people strong and self-reliant."[60] In a "Letter to Satish Chandra Das Gupta" (Camp Hathras, 8 November 1929), Gandhi rejected the selective choice of being violent or non-violent. "The world's history shows that you cannot be violent towards one and non-violent towards another."[61] In a similar letter, he defended *Hind Swaraj.* "We will have to discover a method of dealing with this violence among ourselves. Of course, there is not one word in *Hind Swaraj* that cannot be substantiated. If I have to rewrite it today I may change the language but never the thought."[62] For Gandhi, the characterization of the British Empire was not a sudden decision but based on a painful experience. "The conclusion that the British regime is an evil was arrived at after laborious studies fortified by painful experience. I have set forth the whole process in *Hind Swaraj* as also in *My Experiments with Truth*" ("Letter to K. Natarajan", Sabarmati, 16 May 1931).[63]

Gandhi defended the thesis proposed in *Hind Swaraj* in *A Message to the Aryan Path* (Vol IX, number 9, September 1938), which published a special issue on *Hind Swaraj*. In the revised, new edition of *Hind Swaraj* of 1939, Mahadev Desai attributed the special *Hind Swaraj Number* of the *Aryan Path* "to the devoted labours of that gifted sister Shrimati Shophia Wadia who sent copies of *Hind Swaraj* (*Indian Home Rule*) to numerous friends abroad and invited the most prominent of them to express their views on the book".[64] The editorial and editors of the *Aryan Path* did not miss the significance of satyagraha in *Hind Swaraj*. "The ideas of this small book have changed the hearts of anarchical revolutionaries; why would they not success in changing the hearts of suffering because misguided European humanity? But European thinkers and leaders have first to effect a change in their own hearts; and nothing will aid them in this transmutation like the actual effort of politically minded India to create a social order founded upon the doctrines of Satyagraha which are in the little book, *Hind Swaraj,* and in other writings of Mohandas Karamchand Gandhi . . . "[65] Gandhi also did not miss the opportunity to reiterate his position of defending *Hind Swaraj* while also indicating the co-learning and dismissal of the book. ". . . [T]he stormy thirty years through which I have since passed, I have seen nothing to make me alter the views expounded in it. Let the reader bear in mind that it is a faithful record of conversations I had with workers, one of whom was an avowed anarchist. He should also know that it stopped the rot that was about to set in among some Indians in South Africa. The reader may balance against this the opinion of a dear friend, who alas! is no more, that it was the production of a fool."[66] *CWMG LXVII* invites attention to Mahadev Desai's preface to the 1938 edition of *Hind Swaraj,* in which the statement of Gopal Krishna Gokhale (1866–1915) is mentioned: "When Gokhale saw the translation, on his visit to South Africa in 1912, he thought it is so crude and hastily conceived that he prophesied that Gandhiji would himself destroy the book after spending a year in India."[67]

During his "Speech at the Prayer Meeting" (25 April 1947, Patna), he defended *Hind Swaraj* unequivocally. "I wrote a book called *Hind Swaraj* when I was in South Africa. That was in 1909, that is, 40 years ago. In those days too I held the same views as I do now."[68]

Three Readings of Hind Swaraj

First Reading

Khan Bahadur Shamsuddin Kadri (B.A., Oriental Translator to the Government of Bombay) wrote to the Commissioner on Police, Bombay about *Hind Swaraj* (dated 16 February 1910).[69] This letter or opinion is very terse and direct. "Sir-With reference to your confidential no. 289-P.192 dated the 10th instant, I have the honour to return herewith the Gujarati book called the "Hind Swaraj" and to state that it is of a decidedly objectionable nature especially considering the present disturbed political condition of the country."[70] The editor also wants the rule of Indians in place of the British. Along with a "reader", the "'Editor' is no less anxious to see the rule in India pass from the hands of the British to those of Indians".[71] Since he is a votary of Tolstoy, he highlights the evils of the armed resistance. Gandhi ascribes "all the evils from which India is suffering—plague, famine, poverty, crime, etc to the railways, education, reforms, lawyers, doctors—in fact everything introduced by Englishmen in this country." He is being labelled as crazy for advising to the keep the least contact with the West. "The English have no place in India, says the 'Editor', if they want to bring their hateful civilisation with them into this country. On condition that this civilisation is kept out of India, the English may be allowed to live in the land."[72] The editor disagrees with the reader on the importance of violence and getting concessions out of fear. "It is quite possible," says the editor, "that what Lord Morley has granted has been granted through fear. But what has been gained through fear can be retained only so long as that fear lasts." Therefore, he advocates peaceful means and among them 'passive resistance'.[73]

Furthermore, after examining, Kadri found (no 31, dated 19 February 1910) that *My Experience of Jail, My Second Experience,* and *My Third Experience* by M.K. Gandhi and *Ethical Religion and Religious Ethics* were not objectionable but "written in a pathetic style".[74] Despite finding that *Universal Dawn* (adaptation from mild works of Ruskin) contained nothing objectionable, he quotes "the moral" which is given at the end in the book. "As a general rule, it is wrong for one people to rule another. It is an unnatural thing that the British should rule over [India]."[75] Gandhi opposed the means of violence or industrialization to regain swaraj. "In writing against the militarism and commercialisation which dominate European politics, he says, "Every European nation looks upon the coloured races as its legitimate prey. If they see any such country, they pounce upon it like crow on carrion. There is reason to believe that this is due to their manufactures."[76] In Mustafa Kamil Pasha's speech, Kadri pointed out that "[t]he moral the speaker draws is that the English must go out of Egypt."[77] Most of the sections of the Defence of Socrates (Plato's dialogues on the defence and death of Socrates) remained unobjectionable.

However, "[i]n the short introduction occurs the following sentence in connection with political future of India: When the disease is properly diagnosed and laid bare, and the outer and inner body of India becomes free and clean of disease by means of appropriate remedies, then neither the English nor any other tyrannical bacteria will be able to do any harm to it."[78]

Bombay Government (Letter from the Bombay Government No. 1540, dated 17 March 1910) wanted the prohibition under the Section 18 of the Sea Custom Act 1878 to prohibit the importation of seditious books including *Hind Swarajya*.[79] This is noted by the Home Department Political Branch about the book—"[t]he 'Hind Swarajya' is abstracted and in part translated. It is clearly seditious."[80] J.C. Ker (24 March 1910) forwarded a copy of a report on a Gujarati book entitled *Hind Swarajya*.[81] Some passages were marked. Responding to this, it was highlighted that "This is the first of the pamphlet mentioned in Bombay Government letter No. 1540, dated 17-3-10, which was found in possession of Chibbu Parbhu on his arrival at Bombay from Durban and in respect of which the Bombay Government have asked us to take action under section 19 of the Sea Custom Act.[82] H.C. Woodman and H.A. Stuart "concluded that Mr. M.K. Gandhi is not the innocent martyr as which he poses". It might be advisable to inform the I.O. of this book.[83] Home Department (political, Simla, 28 April 1910) wrote to Sir Richmond Ritche (K.C.B. H.M's U.S. of State for India). J. Filson (Office of the Inspector-General of Police, C.I.D. and Railways, Madras, dated March 18, 1910, M. No. 263) sent a copy of the report of Hind Swarajya by the Gujarati Interpreter to the Madras High Court to J.C. Ker (I.C.S., P.A. to D.C.I. Calcutta). "As it revealed objectionable passage, the local

Government have been addressed with a view to issuing orders prohibiting the importation of the book, under the India Press Act, 1910."[84]

Second Reading

10–15 March 1910 became a significant period for understanding the text through selective translation by the Gujarati translator of Madras High Court and submission. The translator received the text on 10 March 1910 and submitted the selective translation of *Hind Swarajya* on 15 March 1910. Section 12 (1) of the Indian Press Act was invoked by the governments of Bombay, Madras and Bengal for issuing the order for the forfeiture of the text. Sir H.A. Stuart (Secretary of Home Department, Government of India) forwarded the report in form of information to Sir Richmond Ritchie (the Undersecretary of State for India) on 28 April 1910. India Office received the report on 14 May 1910. Subsequently, the report was seen by Sir Richardson (on 29 August 1910), the Committee of Secretary of State for India (in September 1910) and the Council of Secretary of State for India (14 September 1910).[85]

The text of the covering letter that Sir Stuart sent to Sir Richie is as follows:

I am desired to transmit for the information of the Secretary of State a resume of a Gujarati book entitled "Hind Swarajya" written by Mr. M. K. Gandhi, which has been intercepted at Bombay in course of importation into India. The book is said to have been printed at the international Printing Press, Phoenix, Natal, in 1909 and in it Mr. Gandhi represents himself as the Editor of the "Indian Opinion" of Natal. The Bombay and

Bengal Governments have issued orders of forfeiture under section 12(1) of the Indian Press Act.[86]

The 'Report of the Gujarati Interpreter, High Court, Madras, dated 15 March 1910' is an important source of the development. According to the Gujarati Interpreter, the chief interpreter of the High Court was "asked . . . to translate such portions out of it as many affect British Government and submit them . . . in confidence together with . . . opinion . . . "[87] Some of the extracts from the interpreter's summary and free translation of the paras are reproduced below.

The Gujarati interpreter perceived *Hind Swaraj* as India's self-government. Some of the crucial aspects are as follows: Broadly, all Englishmen are not bad. The petition is of no use. Unrest is a healthy option. Swaraj means that the British should leave India. The criticism of Parliament and the prime minister becomes significant. Western civilization is a great curse. Indians have paved the way for the English to rule over them. Indian condition is miserable by modern civilization. Railways, *vakils** and doctors have made Indian conditions miserable. There is no quarrel with Muslims over the issue of cows. Even in the case of dispute, English courts are ruled out from meddling. Vakils and doctors are synonymized with immorality. Hindustan is stated to be a real place of civilization. Despite some defects, swaraj is important. Despite the debate over violence, real swaraj is by Indians without the English. In the struggle for swaraj, passive resistance becomes extremely important. Swadeshi movement should be broadened to include defects of machinery. English is not the language of India. Pain or suffering is inevitable in struggle. Swaraj, satyagraha,

---

* Lawyers.

satyagrahi and duty have become important reference points. For interpreters, since there is advice to not cooperate with the government by way of passive resistance, it should be nipped in the bud. It should be suppressed immediately.

Report of the Gujarati Interpreter, High Court, Madras, 15 March, 1910[88]

Number/ Chapter	Underlined or objectionable sentences/paragraphs with relevant preceding and/or succeeding sentences/ Other relevant parts
2	**The book is styled "Hind Swarajya" meaning 'India Self-Government.' It purports to be written in Gujarati by Mr. M.K. Gandhi and printed in International Printing Press, Phoenix, Natal, in 1909.** **Mr. Gandhi represents himself as the Editor "Indian Opinion" a paper in Natal and expounds his views on swaraj in the form of dialogue between himself as Editor and his Reader who seems to represent the views of young men of the present generation who call themselves Extremeists [Extremists] or Advanced party.**
4	The Editor succeeds in convincing the impatient Reader that he is wrong in his opinion and impresses upon his mind that **all Englishmen are not bad. Some of them are Swaraj's friends.** *Other relevant parts* The substance of the 1st chapter is: In the opinion of the editor, it is the Indian National Congress, Hume, Wedderburn, Gokhale and others who have sown the seeds and prepared the ground for swaraj. To these people India is indebted for the present awakening of swaraj.

5 (Chapter Two: Partition of Bengal)	The real awakening dates from the partition of Bengal . . . **Now the result of this partition is that people have realised that mere petition to King is of no use. It must be supported by strength of endurance of the people.**
5 (Chapter Three: Discontent and Unrest)	The Congress spread discontent among the people according to the advice of Mr. Hume. This discontent has evolved into **unrest** after partition. This **unrest** is a healthy symptom in the opinion of the Editor.
6 (Chapter four: What is swaraj?)	**What is swaraj? - The swaraj that the Reader wants is that the English should leave India but they should leave their constitution, laws and customs and army so that Indians may rule India in their place.** *Other relevant parts* . . . But this kind of swaraj is not liked by the editor and he calls it "Inglastan." He dislikes the English system of Government.
7 (Chapter Five: State of England)	In the opinion of the Editor, the system of government by Parliament is faulty. Although members are selected by people, although best men are sent, yet they are not working with disinterested motives. They do not vote according to their conscience . . . The Prime Minister whoever he may be does not care for governing virtuously. He cares for the success of his party. **He does not care for morals or religion. He is honest, so far as he does not take bribes in the ordinary sense. But he is open to influence. He bribes members to gain his and by giving them title**s. There is no one question which the Parliament has permanently solved. It is a body of talkers and a mere baby after 700 years of existence. It has wasted public time and money.

7 (a)	*Other relevant parts*
	The Englishmen or voters form their views of Government from the Press, which is not an honest one. At one time it advocates one thing, at another time a different thing. They always change their opinions. The Editor strongly condemns this European civilization.
8 (Chapter Six: Civilisation)	In the opinion of the Editor **the Western civilization is a great curse bringing misery upon the masses**.
9 (Chapter Seven)	**The English have not conquered India, but we have the Indians have given over India to them**. They came here to trade. Their object was to get money from India to them and not to govern India . . . Our kings fought among themselves. They asked their assistance and the English gave it. Then Hindus and Mahomedans fought with one another. It is not true that they have conquered it. They are now keeping India, not by sword but by our own cooperation. If we do not cooperate with them, they cannot rule over us. It is not their arms and ammunition that enable them to rule over us. But it is our own interest in their trade that leads us to cooperate with them and hence they rule. Cease cooperation, and they must cease to rule of necessity.
9 (Chapter Eight: State of India)	**The state of India is penniless. It is rendered miserable not by the English, but by the modern civilization . . . What people call happiness of peace by English Government, but I do not see any happiness in this peace. This peace has turned us unmanly and cowardly . . . Instead of leading a cowardly life, it is better to die from the arrows of the Bhils and Pindaries.**

	Other relevant parts
	. . . Macaulay called Indians cowardly. But it denoted his ignorance of the Indians. They are never cowardly. They slept soundly in their fields occupied by tigers and destructive animals. They were always fearless. They were and are brave still.
10 (Chapter Nine: The State of India Continued):	It is the Railways, Vakils and Doctors that have made India miserable. It is quite sure that the English cannot keep so much control as at present without these Railways. **Railways have spread the plague. They have increased famine. Railways have increased wickedness.** It is a mistake to suppose that Railways enable you to hear the united voice of the one nation. It is the English who have impressed upon your mind that India was never one nation, and it would take centuries to become one. It is wrong. **When the English were not in India, we were one nation.**
11 (Chapter Ten: Hindu-Mussulmans)	*Other relevant parts* Hindus and Muhammadans do not cease to become one nation. Religion does not prevent people from becoming one people and living together peacefully . . . It is wrong to suppose that Hindus and Muhammadans cannot become one nation . . . There is nothing like innate enmity between the two races.
12 Cow	**If my brother the Muhammadan** were to follow a different path from mine, why should I quarrel with him. Let him have his own way. **If he a little ignorant, and if I be a little enlightened**, it is my duty to see that quarrel upon this point should not take place between me and my brother.

	Other relevant parts
	I worship the cow, because it is useful animal. Man too is useful. Muhammedans also agree with me in this idea. Our cultivation and prosperity depend upon cows. I would induce my Muhammadan brethren to spare this animal. If they do so well and good. If they do not, I should not fight with my own brother Muhammadan for the sake of the cow. But I would allow me to be sacrificed instead of fighting with my brother . . . If we both brothers are of sound mind, or even if one be of sound mind, the English can never disturb the friendliness between both of us. If they succeed, it is not their fault, but is our fault.
14	I do not mean to say that Hindus and Muhammadans would never fight. **But they should not carry their dispute to the English court and thereby** lower them in their eyes.
15 (Chapter Eleven: State of India continued)	**Vakils- The profession of vakils is one the wicked professions based upon the foundation of immortality and self-aggrandisement . . . The profession ought to be despised and given up. What applies to vakils also applies to Judges. They are brothers.** *Other Relevant Parts* Vakils . . . It is they who have lent support to the British Raj in India sup,ported their supremacy, and enslaved the masses. If Indians cease to become lawyers and . . . [help] . . . the British Courts, the British Raj would come to an end in a single day . . .

16 (Chapter Twelve: State of India)	**Doctors. -It is the profession of the English medicine that has firmly fixed the English yoke on our necks . . . Hospitals are roots of sin. They teach people to take less care of their body and encourage them in their vices. Besides, English Doctors have transgressed the bounds of morality. To give nominal comforts to human body, they are making experiments upon living animals and to torture them and this would hurt the religious feelings of the Hindus, Muhammadans and Parsies . . . This state of things has debased us and rendered us unfit for service to the masses.** Doctors learn this profession to make money and to enrich themselves and not to render any public service. For one penny worth medicine they charge rupees.
17 (Chapter Thirteen: Real Civilization)	**Real civilization** is the one which has survived the lapse of ages and also many other civilizations such as those of ancient Greece, Rome, and other countries. That civilizatio**n is the civilization of Hindustan.**
17	That conduct of life, which enables a human being to control his senses, feelings and passions, to discharge his duties efficiently and to know himself, is real civilization . . . **Such a nation had real swaraj or self-government . . .** In spite of this kind of civilization now prevailing among the ignorant masses of India, **I am conscious that there are some defects too,** such as early marriages, infant widows, one woman having more husbands than one and several other vices.
18 (Chapter Fourteen: How Hind is to get rid of?)	*Other Relevant Parts* Regaining our own civilization is our swaraj, and that is within the palm of our hands. If we the educated people of India free ourselves from slavery, it amounts to freeing the whole of India.

19 (free translation from pages 105–07 of the book)	Now you (meaning of the Reader of Indian Opinion) must have perceived this much that **it is not necessary for us to keep the object of driving away the English**. If the English were to live, becoming Indians, we could accommodate them. If the English want to live with their own civilization, then there is no room for them in India. To bring such a state of things into existence is in our minds. Reader. - I do not like all this talk. There is the least doubt that **we shall have to turn out the English by use of force**. Editor. - In this fit of your passion, you have forgotten all I told you . . . The contempt that you are showing to them deserves to be shown to their civilization. **However, suppose that we might turn them out by making war. How is it possible to do so?** Reader. - **By doing what Italy did. What Mazzini and Garibaldi did, we can also do. Can you deny that they became great heroes?**
20 (Chapter Fifteen: Italy and Hind)	In the opinion of the Editor, Mazzini wanted to give swaraj to the masses or peasantry of Italy and therefore everybody ought to become able to enjoy swaraj. Garibaldi thought otherwise. He wanted to **free Italy from the yoke of Austria anyhow**.
21	*Other Relevant Parts* There are some native states in India who are more oppressive than the English. My patriotism does not teach me that I should allow the masses to be crushed down by the native Kings of India.

22 (Free translation).	**Reader. - You have proceeded too far. It is not necessary to arm all people. First, we would commit several murders and terrify.** Editor. -Your ideas seem to turn the holy land of India into a monstrous one . . . Those who would enjoy sovereignty by committing murders, would never make nation happy. . . . **Those who believe that has resulted from the murder committed by Dhingra and the murder committed in India are committing a great mistake. I consider Dhingara a patriot. But his affection was mad. He has sacrificed in a wrong way. Therefore, at last there is disadvantage.**
25 (Chapter Seventeen: Moral force)	**Editor advocates the use of moral force or passive resistance** against the laws of his country, which one honestly believes to be unjust. He advises people not to obey such laws, and suffer the punishment promoted by such laws. To obey laws which we believe unjust is not the symptom of our fidelity . . . The kings of India have used physical force from time to time to maintain their supremacy. But the nation that is the masses of the cultivators have never done so and will never do. Their highest sword is the two-edged sword of spiritual or moral force or passive resistance. Where subjects use passive resistance against their oppressive King, the King is powerless in spite of his sword. The masses of India have never feared sword and will never fear it. Its great virtue is its fearlessness of death. When the King becomes oppressive, the subjects become angry with the king and that is the moral force of passive resistance.

26 (Moral Force)	*Other Relevant Parts*
	The essential qualities of a "Satyagrahi" (meaning the follower of the truth or the person offering passive resistance) should be "Brahmachariya," that is, leading a life free from lust, freedom from avarice of money, the love of truth and fearlessness"
27 (Chapter Eighteen: Education)	*Other Relevant Parts*
	Education, thereby meaning and reading and writing, is a sort of weapon which can be used with advantage as well as disadvantage.
28	*Other Relevant Parts*
	The knowledge of English is not necessary for *swaraj*. Macaulay who has given us Western Education has made slaves of Western Civilization.
29	*Other Relevant Parts*
	English education has increased vanity, anger, oppression, etc. By a little reflection, it would appear that if we cease taking English education, it would startle the English authorities.
30	*Other Relevant Parts*
	Our education should be through our own vernacular.
31 (Chapter Nineteenth: Machinery)	*Other Relevant Parts*
	They have destroyed Europe and commenced its devastation in India too.
32	**I am delighted to hear of the swadeshi moment in Bengal. But I am sorry that the Bengalis have not included machinery in their boycott. Machines have spoiled the health and morals of workmen.** They have enriched a few who desire the permanency of English Raj in India.

33	*Other Relevant Parts*
	Let their place [machinery] be gradually supplied by hand-made things.
34	*Other Relevant Parts*
	Remove machinery. The effect will be to reduce big cities.
35 (Chapter Twenty)	*Other Relevant Parts*
	I would like to serve the Moderates as well as the Extremists, both the parties. Where I differ from them, I leave them alone, and I would proceed with my work.
36 (Free Translation)	*Other Relevant Parts*
	[To the Extremists] As to 'Swaraj' everyone should take—should make his own. It is not "Swaraj" which another person obtains, but it is 'Per-raj' (that is) foreign-raj. That is to say, if you were to believe that you obtained swaraj by turning out the English, it is not proper . . . [Swaraj cannot be taken] . . . by means of ammunition. Ammunition is not a thing that can agree with Hind. Therefore, depend upon, "Satyagraha" passive resistance. Do not even suspect in mind that ammunition is necessary to obtain 'Swaraj.'
38	*Other Relevant Parts*
	[To the moderates] . . . [M]ere supplication . . . is a disgrace to us.
	We do not want oppression or constraint either by the White or the Hindi

40	Reader. - So much would you tell to both the parties. **What would you tell the English?** Editor . . . But in spite of your being King, you shall have to remain becoming a servant. We will not carry your directions, but **you shall have to carry out our directions.** Until now the wealth that you took away from this country, you have digested. But now you cannot successfully do it. **If you desire to render military services to India, you can remain.**
41	**English is not the language in India, but it is Hindi. You shall have to learn it.** And we can keep correspondence with you in our language alone.
42	After Railways and soldiers, you are spending inexhaustible wealth. We cannot tolerate it. We do not see their necessity. **You might have a fear of Russia. We have not. We do see, when they would come** . . . We would manage with things produced in this country. Your one eye is on Manchester and the other on us. Such a thing we cannot tolerate
43	*Other Relevant Parts* We are not going to help you in doing what we do not like and without our cooperation, you cannot move a step.
47	**Editor. - To this nation I would tell, 'that Indian alone who is rightly intoxicated would be able to tell the English as above and who would not be influenced by their influences.' That person alone would be rightly intoxicated who consciously believe that Indian civilization is a show lasting for three days. Many such civilization came and passed away.**

	(7) who being doctor would understand that in spite of his following any religion, instead of curing a disease by experimenting upon animal life, even if it be so possible to cure, it is advisable to leave it uncured. **(18) All Indians would understand that no nation has raised itself without bearing pain. A trial even in the** battlefield is pain, to kill others is . . . *Other Relevant Parts* That person alone can be rightly intoxicated who would experience moral strength and would remain fearless, not caring for physical strength and who would not even dream to make use of gun power.
48	(1) the Kingdom of our mind is the real 'Swaraj' (2) its key is 'Satyagrahi' (persistence after truth) atmabal (strength of soul) or the power of money" (3) to try the said strength, it is necessary to catch hold of people swadeshi by self-interest (4) **what we want to do is the result of our duty, and not out of enmity towards the English,** not for the purpose of punishing them. That is to say, if the English were to abolish the salt tax, return the wealth already taken, give high offices to all Indians, withdraw the army, then we will make use of their machine- made cloth, use their English language, or make use of their arts. It is not so. All that is not actually worth doing; therefore, we will not do it. So, you must understand. Whatever I have said is not on account of enmity towards the English but on account of enmity towards their civilization that I have said.

50	I have been given sufficient matter to form an opinion on whether it is seditious or not. Nowhere The Author Of The Book Advocates Revolt Or The Use Of Physical Forces Against British Government in India. But he openly advocates passive resistance to subvert British supremacy. **He advises all people not to cooperate with the government.** If this idea takes hold of the minds of young, inexperienced men, it might lead to systematic strikes among Government servants of various classes, as well as public works such as Railway, Post, Telegraph, etc. Surely, it is a very dangerous thought to the safety of the Government. The sooner it is suppressed, the better. The writer has expressed his ideas on other matters which are ridiculous and impracticable. **It only indicates that the perception of the writer seems to be clouded by over-patriotism.**

J. H. Duboulay (Esq., C.I.E., Secretary to the Government of Bombay, Judicial Department) wrote to the Secretary to the Government of India , Home Department (No. 1540; 17 March 1910) regarding the detaining of 415 copies of *Hind Swarajya* (along with seven copies of *Universal Dawn*, seven copies of *Mustafa Kamal Pasha's Speech*, seven copies of the *Defence of Socrates: Story of a True Warrior*, seven copies of *Religion of Morality*, seven copies of *First Experience of Jail*, seven copies of *Second Experience of Jail* and seven copies of *Third Experience of Jail* from Chibba Parbhu in the Custom House. The letter also mentions the selling of four copies on the ship by him, which were also detained by the Customs Authorities[89]. He referred to the two reports (No. 28, dated February 16, 1910, on *Hind Swarajya*;

No. 31, 19 February 1910, on *Universal Dawn, Mustafa Kamal Pasha's Speech*, the *Defence of Socrates: Story of a True Warrior)* by the Oriental Translator to Government for declaring these books objectionable thus inviting forfeiture of the books. "The Governor in Council has accordingly by notification under section 12 of the Indian Press Act, 1910, ordered that these be forfeited to His Majesty . . . [He forwards] . . . a copy of the notification referred to and to request that Government of India may be moved to prohibit the importation of these books under section 19 of the Sea Customs Act, 1878."[90] According to the notification no. 1538 (dated 17 March 1910; signed by J.H. Duboulay; by order of His Excellency the Honourable the Governor in Council), *Hind Swarajaya* and other books were forfeited by section 12 of the Indian Press Act, 1910 (1 Of 1910) for likely to bring into hatred, contempt and disaffection against the Government established by law in British India.[91]

Responding to Duboulay (letter no 1540, dated 17 March 1910), Harold Stuart (K.C.V.O, C.S.I., Secretary to the Government of India, Home Department) did not deem fit to issue an order under section 19 of the Sea Customs Act regarding the prohibition of the importation of the book. "In reply, I am to say that the provisions of sections 13 and 15 of the Press Act enable the Government of Bombay to take all necessary action to prevent the importation of these books into British India and their transmission by post should they succeed in gaining entry. It appears therefore to the Government of India no orders are required under section 19 of the Sea Customs Act."[92] Duboulay made a further request to bring in the Sea Customs Act since the penalty was attached to it (No. 4515, 9 August 1910; letter to Secretary to the Government of India, home Department). ". . . [T]he importation of publications, which are notified under section 19 of the Sea Customs Act, exposes the importer to a fine which may amount to Rs. 1000 but that no penalty attached to the importation of publications which are notified under the Press Act and not under the Customs Act as well."[93] H. G. Stokes (ESQ, Deputy Secretary to the Government of India, Home Department) wrote the letter to him while providing two sets of information (No 990, Calcutta, November 1910): ". . . One showing the seditious publications which the Government of India will now notify and the other showing those publications which have already been notified under section 19 of the Sea Custom Act."[94] In List 1 (a list of publications that the Government of India has now decided to notify under section 9 of the Sea Customs Act), *Hind Swarajya*—a Gujarati book by M.K. Gandhi—was placed at number 5. In List 2 (a list of publications which have already been notified under section 19 of the Sea Customs Act), *Indian Home Rule* is mentioned and placed at serial number 11.[95] Subsequently, Stokes communicated with the Chief Secretary to the Government of United Provinces (No. 42, Calcutta, 25 January 1911) and Robertson's communication with the Director General of the Post Office of India were direction searching copies of seditious literature prohibited under section 19 of the Sea Custom Act, 1878 (VIII of 1878) and especially in the latter appointment of the Director of Criminal Intelligence by the Governor General in Council "as the officer to whom any copies of the publications, which may be found, shall be delivered".[96]

Third Reading

Gandhi's letter to "the Secretary to the Government of India, Home Department, Calcutta" (dated 16 April 1910, Johannesburg) contained a translation of the Gujarati *Hind Swaraj*.[97] This was a clarificatory letter regarding ambiguity around the confiscation of *Hind Swaraj*. Gandhi pointed out his unawareness about the reason for the confiscation of the book. According to Gandhi, "[i]n my humble opinion, every man has a right to hold any opinion he chooses, *and to give effect to it also, so long, he does not use physical violence against anybody.*"[98] Furthermore, "I need hardly say that the views expressed in '*Indian Home Rule*' have nothing whatsoever to do with the struggle that is going on in the Transvaal and in other parts of South Africa, intimately connected though I am with it; and I am not in a position to know how many of my countrymen share those views. At the same time, no matter where I am placed, I consider it my duty to popularize them to the best of my ability as being in the best interest of India and the Empire."[99]

The earliest response (Pro. No. 96, A. L., 27 May 1910) reconfirmed the interception and prohibition. "Mr. Gandhi's translation of his book and the translation made by the Gujarati Interpreter to the Madras High Court are very similar. The worst portions which were marked in the Interpreter's translation have been referred to in Mr. Gandhi's book. The passages on pages 20, 53, 61, 64, 65 and 77 are sufficient to condemn Mr. Gandhi's book."[100] According to H.C. Woodman (31 May 1910), Gandhi does "not in any way improve his case by the preface to his English translation of the book, and in its English form it deserves confiscation as fully as it did in Gujarati".[101]

H.C. Woodman (Additional Deputy Secretary) informed Gandhi about the letter on his English edition of *Hind Swaraj*, which was transferred to the Government of Bombay for disposal[102] (No. 651, Simla, 14 June 1910). The Secretary to the Government of India (Home Department) wrote a letter to the Secretary to the Government of Bombay, Judicial Department (Telegram no. 694, Simla, 5 July 1910). "It is proposed by the Government of India that orders under section 19, Sea Customs

Act, and section 26, Post Office Act, should issue in respect of it."[103] He asked about action taken by the Bombay Government under the Press Act. The Secretary again reminded his Bombay counterpart to act regarding Gandhi's book (Telegram number 726, Simla, 21 July 1910).[104] The reply stated the affirmation of action. "The Bombay Government are notifying book mentioned under section 12 of the Press Act."[105] W. Maxwell (C.I.E., ICS; Secretary to the Government of India, Department of Commerce and Industry) instructed the Director-General of the Post Office of India (No. 5334-1, Simla, 28 July 1910) to intercept postal article "Indian Home Rule" by M.K. Gandhi of Johannesburg, South Africa and to deliver it to the Director of Criminal Intelligence.[106]

Endorsed by the government of India, Department of Commerce and Industry (No. 5335-I), the notification (No. 5348-81, Simla, 30 July 1910) enforced the Sea Customs Act. "In exercise of powers conferred by section 19 of the Sea Customs Act, 1878 (VIII of 1878), the Governor General in Council is pleased to prohibit the bringing by sea or by land, into British India, of any copy of the booklet entitled 'Indian Home rule' by M.K. Gandhi of Johannesburg, South Africa."[107] A copy was also "forwarded to the Government of Bombay, Madras and Burma, Revenue Department, Bengal and Eastern Bengal and Assam, Financial Department . . . the Home Department and . . . Director General of the Post Office of India, for information".[108] (No. 5349-5355-81)

'Statement of publications proscribed in each province under the Indian Press Act, 1910'[109] (May 1913) mentioned the proscription of *Hind Swarajya* in Bombay, Bengal, the United Provinces, Burma and the Central Province.[110] In all these, the book is described as "a Gujarati book by M.K. Gandhi."[111]. Burma, Eastern Bengal and Assam, the Central Province and the North West Frontier

Provinces also mentioned *Indian Home Rule*, "a book in English by M.K. Gandhi"[112]. According to 'list of newspapers, etc, the importation of which into British India is prohibited under section 19 of the Sea Customs Act', '*Hind Swarajya*' is mentioned as "[a] revolutionary book in Gujarati by M.K. Gandhi and printed in Natal"[113] and *Indian Home Rule* as "[a]n objectionable book written by M.K. Gandhi of Johannesburg, South Africa".[114]

The proscription of the book in 1910 was renewed in 1919. The ban was lifted in 1938.

Structure of the Book

In the 1910 edition, the *Preface to the English Translation* (Johannesburg, dated 20 March 1910) and *Foreword* (Kildonan Castle, 22 November 1909) are important components. Gandhi points out the submission of the translation of *Hind Swaraj* to the public. It is a faithful rendition of the original text written in Gujarati. Concerning using the dialogue format for the book, he highlights the prevalent method in the Gujarati language to discuss difficult subjects. Moreover, the dialogue is a discussion among several people. He refers to the masters of the West (Tolstoy, Ruskin, Thoreau, Emerson and others) and Indian philosophy. Tolstoy is considered as one of the teachers. After emphasizing the epistemological plurality, which cut across the dichotomy of the East and the West, he makes the much-invited attentive division between modern and ancient civilization. There are two readings of this description. In the first, the British Government in India was itself a struggle between modern civilization and ancient civilization. Modern civilization is termed as the kingdom of Satan and ancient civilization as the kingdom of God. In the second reading, modern civilization is termed 'the God of war' and ancient civilization as 'the God of love'. Therefore, the struggle become the struggle between war and love, not between people. In this way, Gandhi simply evades the essentialization and caricaturing of people. He opposes the thesis that a civilization based on war and violence can be popular. He does not link people to evil. Herein, Gandhi simply rejects the triad of modern civilization-war-violence. Ancient civilization is synonymized with a trio of anti-war-love and non-violence. In his schema, opposition to violence cannot be recourse to violence. Violence, which is based on the desensitization of human beings, is opposed by love and non-violence. Violence/non-violence become the central concern for the writing of the book.[115]

The foreword in this book was a translation from the Gujarati version written for *Indian Opinion*. His four-month stay in London as part of the Transvaal Indian deputation and meeting with Indians and Englishmen became a significant backdrop for presenting the conclusions. The book was his because he was expected to act on the views, but it was not his because he had no claim of originality. The views were based on a slew of readings. Truth became an important part of this journey. Gandhi was ready to reject any view if it was found contrary to the truth. A dialogue format between the reader and the editor was to facilitate easy reading.[116]

The first Indian edition, 1919, contained a note by C. Rajagopalachari and a new foreword by Gandhi. Rajagopalachari invited attention to violence. There were two sets of votaries of violence. In the case of the first, small, dwindling class, they acted as per their faith. In the second, a large mass believed in violence due to the failure of constitutional agitation, but their belief in violence did not lead to action. Nevertheless, the force became an important source. For him, there was a great evil in these cases. Eradication of force in any form and refutation of violence became very necessary. Therefore, the publication of Gandhi's famous book became extremely important.[117]

Gandhi, in his new foreword, highlights the significance of re-reading and reprinting the book as it is. However, in case of revision, he wished to drop a word, as he had assured his English friend. The word was 'prostitute' used for Parliament. He emphasized swaraj as the only true way. Satyagraha became very important as the law of love, i.e., the law of life. Departure from it was synonymized with disintegration and integration with regeneration.[118]

The years 1919 to 1920 were a transformative period in Indian history, largely due to Gandhi's pivotal role. His and *Hind Swaraj's* emergence were crucial for understanding India's transformation during this time.

This period encompassed the Khilafat movement, non-cooperation, Gandhi becoming indispensable not only for two factions of Muslims, but also linkage between Hindu and Muslim, the unjust treaty of Sèvres with Turkey, the Hunter Commission Majority Report on the Punjab disturbances, Gandhi's promise of "swaraj within one year", Congress becoming a mass organization (by way of a regular four-anna membership; a hierarchy of village-taluka-district or town committees; reorganization of PCCs on a linguistic basis, with the number of delegates to be fixed in proportion to population and a small fifteen-member Working Committee as the real executive head), widespread labour unrest, organization and peasant awakening.[119]

Gandhi spoke on "swaraj in one year" during the resolution on non-cooperation at the special sessions of the Indian National Congress, Calcutta, September 1920 and also wrote in an article "Swaraj in one year" on 22 September 1920 in *Young India*. "Swaraj in one year" was contingent on the sufficient condition for non-co-operation. "Swaraj means a state such that we can maintain our separate existence without the presence of English . . . There can be no swaraj without our feeling and being the equals of Englishmen."[120] He invited attention to the Indian dependence on the Englishmen for internal and external security, armed peace between Hindus and Muslims, education, everyday needs and religious settlement. Rajas and the rich depended on them for power and millions, respectively. The British knew our helplessness. Recovery from helplessness was crucial for achieving swaraj. The *Times* also ridiculed Indians for boycotting the 1920 election as missing an opportunity for training in swaraj.[121] For Gandhi, real freedom/power was not decided in the reformed councils, law courts and governorship. Since the British could not rule us by force, they took recourse to multiple means.[122] The British ". . . want India's billions and . . . India's man power for their imperialistic greed . . . If we refuse to supply them with men and money, we achieve our goal, namely, swaraj, equality, manliness."[123]

Gandhi advocated self-sacrifice by way of non-cooperation. Non-co-operation's commencement was also the beginning of withdrawing support. "If we can but free ourselves from the threefold *maya*† of Government-controlled schools, Government law courts and legislative councils, and truly control our education, regulate our disputes and be indifferent to their legislation, we are ready to govern ourselves and we are only then ready to ask the government servants, whether civil or military, to resign, and the tax-payers to suspend payment of taxes."[124] This was a struggle against brute forces, the isolation of which was necessary.

---

† Illusion.

In this struggle, swadeshi became an important doctrine. "All this means discipline, self-denial, organising ability, confidence and courage."[125]

Gandhi also adhered to his earlier piece while speaking to a *Times* representative, published as "Swaraj in Nine Months" in *Young India* (29 December 1920). Concerning the direction of the non-cooperation movement, he spoke about people's fixed determination and self-sacrifice for the redressal of Khilafat wrongs, the Punjab wrongs and the attainment of swaraj of their choice. He explained his notion, i.e. "swaraj of my ideal". "My swaraj . . . is the Parliamentary government of India in the modern sense of the term of for the time being . . . "[126] Gandhi hoped at the end of nine months, government conditions would be like this: "The lion will then lie with lamb."[127] It is interesting to note the existence of two pointers—time being was an added reminder, and people as sovereign were not relinquished. Gandhi unravelled "The Secret of My Swaraj" by highlighting the importance of economic independence in *Young India* (19 January 2021).[128]

Against this backdrop, Gandhi wrote an article, "Hind Swaraj or the *Indian Home Rule*", on 26 January 1921 in *Young India*. This article became crucial because it was included in the 1921, 1922, 1938 and 1939 editions of *Hind Swaraj*. It contained less than 700 words. Gandhi appreciated *Hind Swaraj* for gaining wider attention. He rejected violence in it and highlighted the backdrop of satyagraha for giving him enough confidence to write *Hind Swaraj*. This book, he stated, was meant for the understanding of all, including a child. It taught love over hate and pitted soul forces against brute forces. He stood by the text, barring a change of word (aka prostitute). However, some of the sentences seem contradictory to Gandhi's own reasoning about *Hind Swaraj*. The following can be identified.

Argument One

But I would warn the reader against thinking that I am today aiming at the swaraj described therein. I know that India is not ripe for it. It may seem an impertinence to say so. But such is my conviction. I am individually working for the self-rule pictured therein. But today my corporate activity is undoubtedly devoted to the attainment of Parliamentary swaraj in accordance with the wishes of the people of India.[129]

Argument Two

I am not aiming at destroying railways or hospitals, though I would certainly welcome their natural destruction. Neither railways nor hospitals are a test of a high and pure civilization. At best they are a necessary evil. Neither adds one inch to the moral stature of a nation. Nor am I aiming at a permanent destruction of law courts, much as I regard it as a "consummation devoutly to be wished for". Still less am I trying to destroy all machinery and mills. It requires a higher simplicity and renunciation than the people are today prepared for.[130]

Argument Three

The only part of the programme which is now being carried out in its entirety is that of non-violence. But I regret to have to confess that even that is not being carried out in the spirit of the book.[131]

Argument Four

I can only answer that Satyagraha is made of sterner stuff. There is nothing reserved and nothing secret in it. A portion of the whole theory of life described in *Hind Swaraj* is undoubtedly being carried into practice. There is no danger attendant upon the whole of it being practised. But it is not right to scare away people by reproducing from my writings passages that are irrelevant to the issue before the country.[132]

The earlier article, "Swaraj in One Year", exhibits optimism, and the second reflects pessimism about attaining the swaraj as per *Hind Swaraj*. It needs a careful reading.

Reading Argument One: Here, Gandhi does not give up the idea of swaraj enshrined in *Hind Swaraj*. Accepting people's wishes for parliamentary swaraj does not mean abandoning swaraj per se. The engagement for parliamentary swaraj is not counter to *Hind Swaraj*. However, treating it as the end of *Hind Swaraj* is a wrong postulation.

Reading Argument Two: He is not abandoning his key position but highlights people's lack of enthusiasm for heterodoxy.

Reading Argument Three: Non-violence should be expanded despite societal constraints and limitations.

Reading Argument Four: In the absence of widespread peers and surrounding support, Gandhi hints at postponing some of the ideas for larger unity. He does not suggest abandoning it. There is a difference between postponing and abandoning.

The incorporation of *Hind Swaraj or the Indian Home Rule* in the subsequent editions is not required due to the absence of the required explanation. Methodologically, *Hind Swaraj* must be treated as one of Gandhi's major texts. The article "Hind Swaraj, or the Indian Home Rule", is part of a large corpus of fragmentary writings. Major texts offer comprehensive interpretation in association with fragmentary writings, a narration of the human condition, the transformation of the human condition and the foundational principles of human society and political community. There could be engagement with one of the objectives as well. In the major texts, there is philosophical or intellectual integrity. This goes beyond descriptive content or empirical detailing. In contrast to major texts, fragmentary writings are reflective writings. Or they carry forward the argument of the major text thus becoming the extension of the latter.[133] Moreover,

> Due to hands-on philosophical needs, fragmentary writings may also appear as separate epithets. It may also be misleading due to very generic statements . . . It may be presented as an 'epistemological departure' of writers. This appends due to the 'delinked theorisation' of writers from major texts. It must be noted that fragmentary writings have no independent existence without major texts. Major texts do exist with or without fragmentary writings, but it cannot be stated about fragmentary writings.[134]

Therefore, the article ("Hind Swaraj or the Indian Home Rule", 26 January 1921) cannot be construed as a generic statement. It may be treated as an epistemological departure or delinked theorization from *Hind Swaraj*. However, it should not be read without the major text. Reading it without *Hind Swaraj* is a profound misreading. Fragmentary writings may be avoided when inserted into major texts.

The grave mistake of treating fragmentary writing as the major text is also visible in Dhananjay Keer's reading of *Hind Swaraj*.

> In the booklet Gandhi condemned [the] Parliamentary democracy but in the preface of 1921 he said that he was working for Parliamentary Swaraj in accordance with the wishes of the people of India. It was a paradox that he should help to introduce a system that he himself considered ruinous. Any yet he asserted that he withdrew nothing from his original booklet.[135]

The mere focus on fragmentary writing also produces a disjunctive understanding of the progression of ideas or the integrity of the concept. Heretofore, Gandhi also defends and rekindles the idea of swaraj, which he enunciates in *Hind Swaraj*. Some of his comments, speeches and reminders on swaraj are aimed at popularizing, expanding and universalizing it. By 23 February 1921 ("The Conditions of Swaraj", *Young India*), Gandhi remained sanguine, establishing swaraj by the following October as the "conditions of swaraj" were ripe. However, he does not forget to "rivet our attention" on the following points:

> (1) Cultivating the spirit of non-violence. (2) Setting up Congress organisations in every village. (3) Introducing the spinning wheel in every home and manufacturing all the cloth required for wants through the village weaver. (4) Collecting as much money as possible. (5) Promoting Hindu-Muslim unity

and (6) Ridding Hinduism of the curse of untouchability and otherwise purifying ourselves by avoiding intoxicating drinks and drugs.[136]

For Gandhi, swaraj has to be earned and cannot even granted by God ("The Shimla Visit", *Young India,* 25 May 1921).[137] It means abandonment of fear of death because it hinders the attaining of swaraj ("The Fear of Death", *Young India,* 13 October 1921).[138] Thus, swaraj is not a free gift. It must be achieved through incessant labour ("Independence", *Young India,* 5 January 1922).[139] ". . . swaraj will not drop from the clouds. It will be the fruit of patience, perseverance, ceaseless toil, courage and intelligent appreciation of the environment"[140]("swaraj or Death", *Young India,* 27 August 1925). Swaraj requires national education and national consciousness ("On the Verge of It", *Young India,* 21 May 1925).[141] swaraj goes beyond personal benefit. It means government by many ("Theft on Railways", *Young India,* 28 July 1921)[142] and based on continuous self-sacrifice ("swaraj or Death", *Young India,* 27 August 27 1925)[143] of self-sacrificing and determined workers ("Sacrifice", *Young India,* 24 June 1926).[144]

Gandhi addresses the meaning of swaraj in the backdrop of his article on "Untouchability and swaraj" in *Young India* (12 June 1924). Herein, he links swaraj to freedom for the most vulnerable sections of society. He proposes to buy peace with Muslims and give peace to Dalits based on the self-respect notion of swaraj. Freedom is needed not only from the British yoke but also from any yoke whatsoever. King Log cannot be exchanged for King Stork.[145] "Interrogatories Answered" (*Young India,* 19 January 1925) cautions against the control by a few and advocates for educating people to control authority.

. . . [R]eal swaraj will come not by the acquisition of authority
by a few but by the acquisition of the capacity by all to resist
authority when it is abused. In other words, swaraj is to be
attained by educating the masses to a sense of their capacity to
regulate and control authority.[146]

People as sovereign become critical, as reflected in "Teachers'
Condition" (*Young India,* 6 August 1925). Self-government
means continuous effort to be independent of government control,
whether it is foreign government or whether it is national. Swaraj
government will be a sorry affair if people look up to it for the
regulation of every detail of life.[147]
In "Mahadev Desai and His Successor" (*Young India,* 1 May 1930),
Gandhi emphasizes the no-distinction-no-discrimination-based
nation of swaraj. For him, ". . . [t]he swaraj of my—our—dream
recognises no race or religious distinctions. Not is it to be the
monopoly of the lettered persons or yet of moneyed men. Swaraj
is to be for all, including the former, but emphatically including
the maimed, the blind, the starving, toiling millions."[148] Gandhi
states in "Poor Man's swaraj" (*Young India,* 26 March 1931) that
the real swaraj is a poor man's swaraj, and to make it *poorna swaraj*
must be an extension of amenities of life for the poor.[149] Swaraj
is the rule of all and the rule of justice. It is not the rule of the
majority community ("Question of Safeguards", *Young India,* 16
April 1931).[150] Room for all schools of honest thought and healthy
public life are indispensable for swaraj ("School Masters and
Lawyers", *Young India,* 17 April 1924),[151] which also includes the
freedom of speech and pen ("Gandhiji's Speech at the A.I.C.C",
15 September 1940; *Harijan,* 29 September 1940).[152] Real swaraj

cannot be without the feeling of all men, women and children ("Gandhiji's Press Statement", *Harijan*, 3 March 1946).[153]

The legacy of the 1921 edition continues in the 1922/1924 editions. The 1922/1924 editions titled *Indian Home Rule* claimed to have been "reprinted with a new foreword by the author". These editions contained C. Rajagopalachari's "Note" and Gandhi's "Foreword" from the 1919 edition. This edition also contained *Hind Swaraj* or the *Indian Home Rule: Reply to Critics,* which is a reprint of "Hind Swaraj or The Indian Home Rule" from *Young India*, 26 January 1921, and was already included in the 1921 edition.

In 1922, another edition by S. Ganesan, Madras, was published. It referred to this edition as the second improved edition and removed all previous forewords or prefaces. The publisher included a nine-page introduction. The writer's name remained absent. The introduction briefly describes Gandhi's Socratic method, plain living and high-thinking philosophy based on the force of truth. Self-rule is essential to avoid tyranny. Satyagraha remains critical for obtaining and maintaining self-rule. The following are explained through extensive quotes from Gandhi.[154]

The 1938 edition, which was the reprint of "Hind Swaraj or Indian Home Rule" as printed in the *Young India* issue of 26 January 1921, included Mahadev Desai's preface (dated 2 February 1938, Wardha) and Gandhi's "A Word of Explanation" and is termed the first edition. Gandhi's message to *Aryan Path* (September 1938) was also made part of it. The revised new edition was published in 1939, with the 1938 contents, with the addition of a preface to the new edition by Mahadev Desai (dated 12 December 1938, Wardha). Desai's publication in *Harijan* concerning the "Hind Swaraj" special number in *Aryan Path* was his new preface to the new edition. He called the *Aryan Path* issue 'an important publication'. It acknowledged the role of Sophia Wadia, who made *Hind Swaraj*'s circulation and acquaintance abroad widespread. Desai's comments are with respect to the articles of Professor Soddy, G. D. H. Cole, C. Delisle Burns, John Middleton Murry, J. D. Beresford, Hugh Fausset, Claude Houghton, Gerald Heard and Irene Rathbone. They were pacificists and socialists. Responding to the criticism of the feasibility of non-violence, which was common in all, Desai attributed love as a fundamental condition of non-violence and purity of mind and body as an essential condition for pure, unselfish love. For reviewers, the "attack on machinery and civilisation" by Gandhi was an "unwarranted condemnation of machinery". To this, Desai suggested that "[t]he machine is, like the body, useful if and only to the extent that it subserves the growth of the soul."[155] Concerning the limitation of the doctrine of non-violence, Desai reiterated that "[f]or violence breeds the results of violence, and once you start the game there is no limit to be drawn".[156] In the preface, which was also part of the 1938 edition, Desai stated that Gandhi had translated the book for Kallenbach. The English translation was a response to the proscription by the Bombay Government. Gokhale was not impressed by the English version of the book and thought that this crudely and hastily conceived book would be eventually destroyed by Gandhi after spending a year in India. In Desai's conclusion, the book represented the twin principles of truth and non-violence.[157] It is to be noted that the revised new edition of 1939 (the first edition in 1938) of *Hind Swaraj* or *Indian Home Rule* removed the previous preface, notes and forewords except for the reprint article of *Young India*, 26 January 1921. This was retitled as "A Word of Explanation".

1910 Edition	1919 Edition	1921 Edition	1922/1924 Editions	1922 ('second improved edition')	1939 Revised New Edition (revised of 1938 Edition)
Indian Home Rule by M.K. Gandhi Being a translation of "Hind Swaraj" (Indian Home Rule), published in the Gujarati columns of *Indian Opinion*, 11 and 18 December 1909.	*Indian Home Rule* by M.K. Gandhi Reprinted with a new foreword by the author	*Hind Swaraj* or *Indian Home Rule*, by M.K. Gandhi	*Indian Home Rule* by M.K. Gandhi Reprinted with a new foreword by the author	*Indian Home Rule* by M.K. Gandhi	*Hind Swaraj* or *Indian Home Rule*, by M.K. Gandhi
International Printing Press, Phoenix, Natal, 1910	Ganesh & Co., Madras, 1919	G.A Natesan & Co. Madras, 1921	Ganesh & Co., Madras, 1922	S. Ganesan, Madras	Navajivan Publishing House, Ahmedabad

	Preface to the New Edition by Mahadev Desai An important Publication [comment on the Aryan Path content] The Attack on Machinery and Civilization Limitations of the Doctrine Preface by Mahadev Desai (1938)	A Word of Explanation by M.K. Gandhi, Young India, (26 January 1921)	A Message by M.K. Gandhi (reproduced from the Aryan Path, September 1938)
	Introduction (nine-page introduction by the publisher)	Note by C. Rajagopalachari (Satyagraha Sabha, Madras, 6 June 1919)	Hind Swaraj or the Indian Home Rule: Reply to Critics by M.K. Gandhi, Young India, (26 January 1921)
	Hind Swaraj or The Indian Home Rule by M.K. Gandhi (published in Young India, 26 January 1921)	Foreword by M.K. Gandhi (Bombay, 28 May 1919)	
	Note by C. Rajagopalachari (Satyagraha Sabha, Madras, 6 June 1919)	Foreword by M.K. Gandhi (Bombay, 28 May 1919)	
Preface to The English Translation by M.K. Gandhi, (Johannesburg, 20 March 1910) Foreword Kildonan Castle, (22 November 1910)			

Contents

Weltanschauung of Twenty (plus one) Books

Gandhi enlists twenty books in *Hind Swaraj's* Appendices. These books are crucial to understanding Gandhi's philosophy. These books have convergences and divergences. The most crucial aspect of these books is an emphasis on celebrating heterodoxy in the form of offering nuanced critiques of prevalent conditions. This heterodoxy is backed by the principle of reconciliation of human beings and the principle of antagonism against unjust structures and laws. In other words, heterodoxy combines the principle of reconciliation of beings and the principle of antagonism against unjust structures.

Leo Tolstoy (1828–1910)

The Kingdom of God is Within You (1894): Leo Tolstoy takes this title from Luke 17:21 of the Bible. Reading both Luke 17: 20 and 21 makes the complete meaning. "Once, having been asked by the Pharisees when the kingdom of God would come, Jesus replied, "The kingdom of God does not come with your careful observation [Luke 17: 20], nor will people say, 'here is,' or 'There it is,' because of the kingdom of God is within you [Luke 17: 21]."[158] This verse also helps Tolstoy to develop a non-institutionalized religion. He appeals to freethinking writers to perceive Christ not only as an establisher of religion but also as a reformer.

> I expected that the freethinking writers would look upon Christ not only as the establisher of a religion of worship and personal salvation (as which the ecclesiastics understand him), but, to express myself in their language, as a reformer, who destroys the old, and gives the new foundations of life, the reform of which is not yet accomplished, but continues until the present.[159]

Moreover, Tolstoy proposes non-resistance, which means resistance based on non-violence. "True non-resistance is the one true resistance to evil. It kills and finally destroys the evil sentiment . . . Besides, in general, where non-resistance costs the sacrifice of one life, or the sacrifice of some essential good of life, resistance costs thousands of such sacrifices . . . Non-resistance preserves, resistance destroys."[160] This is an important formulation for satyagraha. Concerning violence, "[i]t is incomparably safer to act justly than unjustly; to bear an insult than to resist it with violence—it is safer even in relation to the present life. If all men did not resist evil with evil, the world would be blessed."[161]

In a "Letter to Manilal Gandhi" (25 March 1909), Gandhi praises *Kingdom* as the most logical book and Tolstoy for the synthesis between practices and preachings.[162] Gandhi's lengthy "Speech on the Birth Centenary of Tolstoy" (10 September 1928) is remarkable in many ways, such as its linkage with Western tradition and Indian tradition. Gandhi's remarkable interpretative ability links myriad sources together. For Gandhi, among Tolstoy's ". . . works the one which has had the greatest effect on . . . [him] . . . is *The Kingdom of God Is Within You*".[163] He borrows the non-violence theory from Tolstoy. "I attach importance to two things in his life. He did what he preached. His simplicity was extraordinary; it was not merely outward; outward simplicity of course he had . . . Tolstoy was a great advocate of non-violence in his age."[164] "Non-violence means an ocean of compassion, it means shedding from us every trace of ill-will for others. It does not mean abjectness or timidity or fleeing in fear. It means, on the contrary, firmness of mind and courage, a resolute spirit."[165]

In addition to non-violence, bread labour (earning bread by labour) is an important aspect of Tolstoy's writing, which he borrows from another Russian writer, T.M. Bondarev. Gandhi brings Tolstoy, the Gita and bread labour together in this speech. Gandhi states that "[t]he cause of the inequalities we see in the world, of the contrasts of wealth and poverty, lies in the fact that we have forgotten the law of life. That law is the law of 'bread labour'."[166] Herein, he referred to Gita's *yajna*‡ as bread labour.

> On the authority of Chapter III of the Gita, I call it *yajna*. The Gita says that he who eats without performing *yajna* is a thief and sinner. Tolstoy has said the same thing. We should not distort the meaning of "bread labour" and forget the real idea. Its simple meaning is that he has no right to eat who does not bend his body and work. If every one of us did bodily labour to earn his food, we would not see the poverty which we find in the world.[167]

He suggests three learnings from Tolstoy's life. The first is defining and achieving swaraj by people, which is not contingent upon the government. Youth ". . . have to choose between two paths in life: one of self-indulgence and the other of self-restraint. Swaraj is not something to be won from the Government . . . [T]he key to swaraj is in our hands, and not in England nor in Simla nor in Delhi. It is in your pocket and mine".[168] The second is concerned with "the pursuit of truth".

> Let us resolve that we will never give up the pursuit of truth. To follow truth, the only right path in this world is that of non-violence. Non-violence means an ocean of love, whose vastness no one has ever been able to measure. If it fills us we would be

‡ Sacrifice.

so large-hearted that we would have room in it for the whole world.[169]

This is bread labour – *yajna*. "We earn the right to eat only by putting the body to hard work, by doing physical labour. Yajna means any work done for the service of others."[170]

Tolstoy is writ large in *Satyagraha in South Africa* from passive resistance to Tolstoy Farm. However, the reference is missing. This is even though "*The Kingdom of God Is Within You* was mandatory reading for members of the Phoenix Settlement".[171] Gandhi acknowledges *The Kingdom of God is Within You* twice in his *Autobiography*. In the first instance, he clubbed Raychandanbhai, Tolstoy and Ruskin together. "Three moderns have left a deep impress on my life, and captivated me: Raychandanbhai by his living contact; Tolstoy by his book, *The Kingdom of God Is Within You* and Ruskin by his *Unto This Last*."[172] In the second instance, he becomes very specific about the value of the book. "Tolstoy's *The Kingdom of God Is within You* overwhelmed me. It left an abiding impression on me. Before the independent thinking, profound morality, and the truthfulness of this book, all the books given me by Mr. Coates seemed to pale into insignificance"[173].

Significance for Hind Swaraj/ Gandhian Philosophy: Non-violence, act for swaraj, symmetry between means and ends, Truth, morality, bread labour, East and West synthesis.

What is Art? (1904): Besides references in appendices of *Hind Swaraj*, the book is not mentioned in *Satyagraha in South Africa* or *Autobiography*. This dense book offers several insights. A few can be reasoned out. Tolstoy uses art to unite people rather than to fragment them. Against the divisiveness in religions, "Christian unity" is used to unite people. Art is also a medium of expression of emotion. For Tolstoy, art has a wider meaning. Before discussing what art is, he describes what art is not. Concerning the first, Tolstoy states that:

> Art is not, as the metaphysicians say, the manifestation of some mysterious Idea of beauty, or God; it is not, as the aesthetical physiologists say, a game in which man lets off his excess of stored-up energy; it is not the expression of man's emotions by external signs; it is not the production of pleasing objects; and, above all, it is not pleasure . . . [174]

The context of the second, "[i]n order correctly to define art, it is necessary, first of all, to cease to consider it as a means to pleasure and to consider it as one of the conditions of human life."[175] "Art is a human activity . . . that one man consciously . . . hands on to others feelings he has lived through, and that other people are infected by these feelings, and also experience them."[176] Positively, art ". . . is a means of union among men, joining them together in the same feelings, and indispensable for the life and progress towards the well-being of individuals and of humanity".[177] Tolstoy remains sanguine about art as inclusiveness of feelings and universality.

> The only subject-matter of the art of the future will be either feelings drawing men towards union, or such as already unite them; and the forms of art will be such as will be open to everyone. And therefore, the ideal of excellence in the future will not be the exclusiveness of feeling, accessible only to some, but, on the contrary, its universality.[178]

In a "Letter to Maninlal and Sushila Gandhi" (5 December 1927), Gandhi draws attention to art. He requests Sushila to not make a distinction between indigenous and foreign in the realm of art. According to Gandhi, "[n]ot everything which appeals to the eye is art . . . I have read conflicting opinions about many paintings and statues expressed by art-critics who have become famous in the world. We should, therefore, think what art means."[179] In this backdrop, Gandhi advises Sushila to read *What is Art?* which is already translated into Gujarati.[180]

Significance for Hind Swaraj/ Gandhian Philosophy: developing and expanding the notion of fellow feelings; moving away from the empiricist notion of pleasure.

The Slavery of Our Times (1900): Gandhi does not mention it in *Satyagraha in South Africa* and *Autobiography*. The influence of the text on Gandhi is profound and has been significantly modified. The text critically problematizes the modern notion of law, which Tolstoy links with "organized violence". *"Laws are rules, made by people who govern by means of organised violence, for non-compliance with which the non-complier is subjected to blows, to loss of liberty, or even to being murdered."*[181] However, life is possible without organized violence. "And, therefore, there is no reason to anticipate men; that people will not be able to arrange their lives without organised violence."[182] Tolstoy does not agree with the postulation that those governing are superior in nature. "Why ought people to be subject to the violence of just those men who are in power at a given time? What proves that these people are wiser than those on whom they inflict violence?"[183] He offers a reasonable agreement over organized violence. It is said, "How can people live without Governments, i.e. without violence?" But it should, on the contrary, be asked, "How can rational people live, acknowledging the vital bond of their social life to be violence and not reasonable agreement?"[184] Reason becomes an important substitute for violence and power. "But if men are rational beings,

then their relations should be based on reason and not on the violence of those who happen to have seized power. And in that case, again, governmental violence has no justification".[185]
Tolstoy equates "existing order" with brute force.

> Between the existing order, based on brute force, and the ideal of a society based on reasonable agreement confirmed by custom, there are an infinite number of steps, which mankind is ascending, and the approach to the ideal is only accomplished to the extent to which people free themselves from participation in violence, from taking advantage of it, and from being accustomed to it.[186]

Reasoning and the voice of conscience are inalienable. "The conclusion to which general reasoning should bring us, is thus confirmed to each individual, by that supreme and unimpeachable judge, the voice of conscience."[187] Tolstoy focuses sharply on laws and legislation, and shows how such laws lead to slavery. "Laws are framed, and repealed, by human beings so that it is not some sociological 'iron' law, but ordinary man-made law, that produces slavery."[188] "Thus the fundamental cause of slavery is legislation : the fact that there are people who have the power to make laws."[189]

In the book, India, Parliament and Transvaal also appear. The money collected from people goes to war. Gandhi's notion of Parliament and Tolstoy's comment on Parliament are interestingly similar.

> The same thing goes on not only in Persia, Turkey, and India, but also in all the Christian and constitutional States and democratic Republics; money is taken from the majority of the people, quite independently of the consent or no consent of the

payers, and the amount collected is not what is really needful, but as much as can be got (we know how Parliaments are made up, and how little they represent the will of the people), and it is used not for the common advantage, but for things the. governing classes consider necessary for themselves: on wars in Cuba or the Philippines, on taking and keeping the riches of the Transvaal, and so forth. So that the explanation that people must pay taxes because they are instituted with general consent and are used for the common good, is as unjust as the other explanation, that private property in land is established to encourage agriculture.[190]

Significance for Hind Swaraj/ Gandhian Philosophy: Higher law and lower law, conscience, Parliament, violence, brute forces, and soul force, dialogical self.

The First Step: An Essay on the Morals of Diet (1891): This is a noticeably short and interesting text by Tolstoy that invites attention to the morality of pleasure in diets. The good life is the prohibition of the usage of labour of others.

> . . . [I]t should surely be clear to every one that a man who uses for his own pleasure (which he might easily forego) the labour, often the painful labour, of others, behaves badly; and that this is the very first wrong action he must cease to commit if he wishes to live a good life.[191]

Augmentation of one's want is a sign of civilization. "According to the prevailing and most widely spread teaching of life to-day, the augmentation of one's wants is, on the contrary, regarded as a desirable condition; as a sign of development, civilization, culture, and perfection."[192] However, a luxurious life and a righteous life are antithetical. "It is impossible for a man living in luxury to lead a righteous life."[193]

Self, others and labour are critical components of his philosophy. "The less there is of love for self, with all the ensuing care about self and the selfish demands made upon the labour of others, and the more there is of love for others, with the resultant care for and labour bestowed upon others, the better is the life."[194] It is important to contribute to others and less for oneself. "The more a man gives to others and the less he demands for himself, the better he is: the less he gives to others and the more he demands for himself, the worse he is."[195]

Hereafter, he focuses on consumption and overeating and the denial of a surplus of food to the needy. "Instead of feeding others a man eats too much himself; by so doing he not only diminishes the possibility of giving away the surplus, but, by over-eating, he deprives himself of power to help others."[196] A luxurious life denies laborious work.[197] Doing good and ceasing from evil both are critical.[198] Tolstoy criticizes a particular form of parasitical luxurious life at the cost of innumerable working and toiling classes. It poses a great challenge to a moral person.

> A moral man, living a life of comfort, a man even of the middle class (I will not speak of the upper classes, who daily consume to satisfy their caprices the results of hundreds of working days), cannot live quietly, knowing that all that he is using is produced by the labour and crushed lives of working-people, who are dying without hope . . . employed in mines, factories, and at agricultural labour, producing the articles that he uses.[199]

His moral appeal to the consuming class is linked to the precarious condition of the working class (working people). The consumption of one class is linked to the massive poverty of working people. He proposes two conditions. First,

> At the present moment I, who am writing this, and you who will read it, whoever you may be, both you and I have wholesome, sufficient, perhaps abundant and luxurious food, pure, warm air to breathe, winter and summer clothing, various recreations, and, most important of all, we have leisure by day and undisturbed repose at night.[200]

Second,

> And here, by our side, live the working people, who have neither wholesome food, nor healthy lodgings, nor sufficient clothing, nor recreations, and who, above all, are deprived not only of leisure, but even of rest : old men, children, women, worn out by labour, by sleepless nights, by disease, who spend their whole lives providing for us those articles of comfort and luxury which they do not possess, and which are for us not necessities, but superfluities.[201]

A moral person must discard articles produced in this condition. "Therefore, a moral man, I do not say a Christian, but simply a man professing humane views or merely justice, cannot but wish to change his life and cease to use articles of luxury produced under such conditions."[202]

Abstinence becomes the condition for a righteous life.[203] Herein, desire is subordination to reasonlessness. "Abstinence is the liberation of man from desires,—their subordination to reasonableness . . . "[204] Abstinence is contingent on fasting. "And yet, just as the first condition of a good life is abstinence, so the first condition of a life of abstinence is fasting."[205] He proposes a certain order of good action for a good life. This sequence is vital for abstinence and self-renunciation: abstinence in food, followed by fasting. Herein, he emphasizes vegetarianism for a good life, meaning abstaining from ". . . animal food, because, to say nothing of the excitation of the passions caused by such food, its use is simply immoral, as it involves the performance of an act which is contrary to the moral feeling—killing; and is called forth only by greediness, and the desire for tasty food".[206] *The Ethics of Diet* is for the previously mentioned reasoning.[207]

Significance for Hind Swaraj/ Gandhian Philosophy: Self-Other, Controlling Palate, rejection of consumption-driven being, abstinence from animal food, vegetarianism, fasting, the plight of working people linked to excessive consumption by the middle and upper class.

How Shall We Escape (1898): This is a short but powerful essay about escaping the slavery of peasants and the working class, which originated due to land dispossession and working under the atrocious conditions of factories. He highlights the importance of the conditions wherein land does not belong to those who work on it but to those who do not work on it. "[W]hy the land does not belong to those who work it, but to those young gentlemen who play about in fancy shirts and drink tea and eat cakes."[208] He further explains the irony. The condition of labourers is that they ". . . overwork themselves for idle, rich landlords; suffer from rupture, asthma, consumption; drink in despair; and die before their time. Women overstrain themselves, cooking, washing, mending, tending the cattle; wither, and grow prematurely old, from overpowering and incessant labor".[209] Contrary to this,

. . . everywhere those for whom they work indulge in horses and carriages and pet dogs, conservatories and games, from one year to another; each day from morning till evening dressing as if for a holiday, playing, eating and drinking, as not one of those who work for them could do, even on a holiday.[210]

In addition to dispossession and exploitation, their consumption and need patterns also make their condition vulnerable. He suggests the right to land to tillers as the air or sunlight. However, it can be changed due to power remaining in the hands of landowners. The cause of slavery of the working classes is land rights in the hands of non-labouring landowners, direct and indirect taxes and defence and upholding of capitalistic property rights. These cannot be changed due to the government's monopoly on violence. He urges people to withdraw from participation in violence, particularly martial-based organizations. Government actions lead to the existence of violence, which is based on "spoliation of the people", the distribution of stolen money to those who organize robbery and martial recruitment. In addition to withdrawing from participation in violence, being conscious of truth and acting according to it becomes essential escape methods.[211]

Significance for Hind Swaraj/ Gandhian Philosophy: against exploiting workers and the working class, refusing to participate in violence and acting according to a conscience of truth.

A Letter to a Hindoo (1908): As discussed earlier, this text was crucial to establishing the relationship between Tolstoy and Gandhi. After the subsequent permission to publish, Gandhi also wrote the preface to the text[212] and subsequently sent copies of the text to him as communicated on Tolstoy on 4 April 1910.[213] Gandhi's two prefaces to *A Letter to a Hindoo* (remained unpublished due to disagreement with the editor of

Free Hindustan, Tarak Nath Das; the letter is dated 14 December 1908) were for Gujarati and English editions. The first preface is for Gujarati translation (S. S. Kildonan Castle, 18 November 1909). Gandhi calls him a "valiant soldier". Being vengeful is the core of the political process, which is wrong. Tolstoy "believes that to return injury for injury does harm both to ourselves and our enemy . . . He is uncompromising in his loyalty to the principle of returning good for evil."[214] Submission to tyranny is ruled out. Submission to injustice is slavery. "Slavery consists in submitting to an unjust order, not in suffering ourselves to be kicked. Real courage and humanity consist in not returning a kick for a kick. This is the core of Tolstoy's teaching."[215]

Tolstoy's letter is of immense value to Gandhi for satyagraha. He draws attention to sources from multi-religious pluralism and its place in Tolstoy's teaching concerning the struggle of love forces against brute force. He uses modern civilization to highlight the significance of Tolstoy and satyagraha.

> But those who have not known what a happy experience satyagraha can be, who have been caught up in the toils of this huge sham of modern civilization, like moths flitting round a flame, will find no interest in Tolstoy's letter all at once. Such men should pause for a moment and reflect.[216]

Indians replacing the British is not ideal if the Indians plan to imitate the British. "Tolstoy gives a simple answer to those Indians who appear impatient to drive the whites out of India . . . The whites cannot remain if we do not want them."[217] Gandhi points out that since Tolstoy addresses his letter to a Hindu, there are citations from Hindu scriptures. All religions contain principles of ethics. Despite not agreeing with all the ideas of Tolstoy, Gandhi adheres to the central principle teaching of Tolstoy.[218] Gandhi suggests that there are no superstitions in Tolstoy's teaching. He highlights the problem of converting the irreligious to religion. Gandhi aimed for a larger Gujarati readership of this text while simplifying the language.[219]

The second preface is to the English edition (S. S. Kildonan Castle, 19 November 1909). In it, he considers Tolstoy as one of his guides.[220] Each Indian has national aspirations against the backdrop of many opinions and many nationalities. There are vivid opinions about the meaning of aspirations and the method of achieving them.

> One of the accepted and "time-honoured" methods to attain the end is that of violence . . . Tolstoy's life has been devoted to replacing the method of violence for removing tyranny or securing reform by the method of non-resistance to evil. He would meet hatred expressed in violence by love expressed in self-suffering. He admits of no exception to whittle down this great and divine law of Love. He applies it to all the problems that worry mankind.[221]

Reproduction of civilization is construed as a reproduction of gun factories and hateful industrialism in India.[222]

"If we do not want the English in India, we must pay the price."[223] As Tolstoy indicates,

> Do not resist evil, but also yourselves participate not in evil, in the violent deeds of the administration of the law courts, the collection of taxes and, what is more important, of the soldiers, and no one in the world will enslave you, passionately declares the sage of Yasnaya Polyana. Who can question the truth of

what he says in the following: A commercial company enslaved a nation comprising 200 millions. Tell this to a man free from superstition and he will fail to grasp what these words mean. What does it mean that thirty thousand people, not athletes but rather weak and ill-looking, have enslaved 200 millions of vigorous, clever, strong, freedom-loving people? Do not the figures make it clear that not the English but the Indians have enslaved themselves?[224]

. . . [t]he central truth of his indictment of the present system . . . is to understand and act upon the irresistible power of the soul over the body, of love, which is an attribute of the soul, over the brute or body force generated by the stirring up in us of evil passions.[225]

Significance for Hind Swaraj/ Gandhian Philosophy: principle of injury and harm, satyagraha, disobedience against tyranny, not eye for an eye, multi-religious pluralism, modern civilisation as a site of violence, non-participation in evil or injustice.

Robert Sherard (1861–1943)

The White Slaves of England (1897): Gandhi does not cite this work often in his writings. However, the influence of the work is impactful. Robert Sherard sketches out the miserable conditions of working people in England.

There is no pleasure in their lives, as in the following pages is so often set forth in their own words; they have no time for relaxation; when in work and when out of work—playing !— their entire energy is taken up in the hunting of the loaf. Living lives far worse than the lives of domestic animals . . . [226]

To highlight the nature of the "worst paid and most murderous trade of England", he "visited six manufacturing centres in the Northern and Midland counties of England . . . "[227] He spent time in the society of workmen, their clubs, the public houses, the workhouses, hospitals, workshops and cottages. He avoided contact with the masters. He visited factories as a trespasser.[228]

His visit to each of the six sites presents the miserable condition of male and female workers. They are subject to low wages, long working hours, health hazards and deteriorating overall beings. At the site, the alkali workers, "[t]here is no Sunday, not even Christmas Day, for the alkali workers when trade is busy."[229] The miserable condition continues in the absence of regularity of work.

> Miserable as the wages are, earned at such risks and with such real physical exhaustion and suffering, the men would yet be contented could they rely on any regularity of work. But they cannot. They are the sport of the markets. Sometimes trade is so slack that they must loaf about idle for weeks and weeks.[230]

At the nailmakers of Bromsgrove, "[t]he industry of nailmaking is profitable only to those who do not make them."[231] The slipper-makers and tailors of Leeds also present a grim condition for workers. According to an old slipper-maker, "[t]here's no such thing as pleasure for me. I go from my bed to my seat, and from my seat to my bed, though now and again I may get, say, an hour over my paper."[232] The girl faces more brutality from the foreman.[233] For Sherard,

> The fearful competition in these trades is, no doubt, to a great extent, the cause of the sufferings of these unfortunate workers.

Yet this consideration will not render comfortable, to the man of heart who has seen the tears of the women, and the gaunt despair of the men, the lounge coat and fireside slippers, which have been made to the tears of those and of these the gaunt despair.[234]

The woolcombers are considered unskilled labourers. They are completely dependent on the employer, thus leading to anxiety about employment.[235] Wages are abysmally low, forcing husband and wife to work different shifts at the workplace. "So poor are the wages, that in hundreds of families of woolcombers in Bradford both husband and wife have to work in the factories, the husband at night, the wife by day."[236] The condition at The white-lead workers of Newcastle does not give much hope. "Women . . . are physically far more liable to lead-poisoning than men, and the consequences of lead-poisoning are far worse in their case."[237] The disease follows the work.

Imagine a life where intermittent periods of all the most painful diseases are inevitable. "Two months on," said a girl to me, "and one month off with sickness is my average". In the end there are paralysis, partial or total blindness, and insanity to be looked forward to by those who stick to their work, because they know no other trade.[238]

At the chainmakers of Cradley Heath, "[t]he work is unhealthy and dangerous."[239] "There are here factories where meagre little girls and boys . . . are put to task, during their apprenticeship, against which a man would revolt.[240] Overall, Sherard summarizes his arguments are as follows:

. . . before my spiritual eyes there passed the pale procession of the White Slaves of England, I could see nothing but sorrow and hunger and grime, rags, foul food, open sores and movements incessant, instinctive yet laborious—an anvil and a hammer ever descending—all vague, and in a mist as yet unlinked with red, a spectacle so hideous that I gladly shut it out, wondering, for my part, what in these things is right.[241]

Significance for Hind Swaraj/ Gandhian Philosophy: modern civilization has led to the vulnerable condition of male and female workers.

Edward Carpenter (1844–1929)

Civilisation: Its Cause and Cure (1889): Edward Carpenter discusses civilization profusely in the book. Civilization is a peculiar state of society. "Some of us, indeed, are inclined to think that it is a kind of disease which the various races of man have to pass through—as children pass."[242] Doctors are also mentioned in connection with disease. National sickness has increased to be attended to by 23,000 medical doctors. It is a serious development.

And *they* do not cure us . . . The state of modern civilised man in this respect- our coughs, colds, mufflers, dread of a waft of chill air etc- is anything but creditable, and it seems to be the fact that, notwithstanding all our libraries of medical science, our knowledges, arts, and appliances of life, we are actually less capable of taking care of ourselves than the animals are.[243]

The physical unity constitutes health, and its absence causes disease. In modern life, unity has disappeared, which also forms true society.[244] A civilized society is under attack in Carpenter. "If the word disease is applicable anywhere, I should say it is—both in its direct and its derived sense—to the civilised societies of to-day."[245] Civilization, division of property and class government are intertwined. "We are justified therefore in calling Civilisation a historical stage, whose commencement dates roughly from the division of society into classes founded on property and the adoption of class government."[246] He perceives a tribal society as ideal because members of a tribe do not fight against each other, and there is an honesty and an absence of class divisions. Loss of unity is a disease physically or mentally applicable to society or individuals. The modern notion of health is a negative one due to the focus on the absence of the disease. The older notion of life is human itself.[247] He rejects the separation between mind and body. Disease is the breaking of unity into multiplicity. He criticizes making the disease a fetish. Heath is unity and integration against disintegration.[248] He defines the unity as "self-knowledge— (which involves in a sense the abandonment of self) . . . conscious of . . . destiny—to lay hold of and realise . . . own freedom and blessedness—to transfer . . . consciousness from the outer and mortal part of . . . [being] . . . to the inner and undying."[249]

Earlier, human beings were in harmony and closer to nature. Disunion of the outer self from the inner causes the worst dual self-consciousness. Civilization, based on property, disintegrates humans and corrupts them. Hitherto, undifferentiated love and desire get separated. The role of property is extremely important. The increase in property growth and power of production draw humans away from nature, their true self and their fellows. The disintegration of humans is caused by the growth of property. Herein, the role and rise of government become important. Accumulation of private property causes the arrival of artificial laws for the maintenance of unequal levels. Force becomes important, so that property owners can use it against non-owners legally. "Each for himself" is not a democracy. True democracy is not an external rule but an inward rule, i.e., the rule of mass-man in each unit-man. Life is a natural space that is worth living. There is no antagonism between humans and nature. There is no need for private accumulation. Men and women cannot be tied to slavery. Work will be done with likes and usefulness, not with wages and rewards. This is the communism hated by civilization. Alongside the movement of civilization, there is a global urge to establish socialistic and communal life on a wider scale.[250] "It is in these two movements—towards a complex human Communism and towards individual freedom and Savagery—in some sort balancing and correcting each other, and both visibly growing up within—though utterly foreign to—our present-day Civilisation, that, we have fair grounds I think for looking forward to its cure."[251]

He does not approve of the delinking of the logical and intellectual parts of human beings from the emotional instinct. Approximation of truths needs to be revisited along with an understanding of the phenomenon of living beings, which is more complex than astronomy or physics. There cannot be kept feeling out of fact.[252] "In the individual, feeling precedes thinking . . . "[253] To know the destination of humans (the word *man* is used), astronomy, biology, physics, ethics, etc, are required.[254] Local consciousness is linked with the universal consciousness.[255] He questions the set pattern of morality. "On the whole we pride ourselves (and justly, I believe) on the general advance in humanity; yet we know that to-day the merest savages can only shudder at a civilisation whose public opinion allows—as amongst us—the rich to wallow in their wealth while the poor are systematically starving . . . "[256] Law is linked with ruling classes thus acquired respectability. "Law represents from age to age the code of the dominant or ruling class, slowly accumulated, no doubt, and slowly modified, but always added to and always administered by the ruling class. To-day the code of the dominant class may perhaps best be denoted by the word Respectability . . . "[257] Respectability, property and justice are intertwined. "The respectability of to-day is the respectability of property. There is nothing so respectable as being well-off." "The Law confirms this: everything is on the side of the rich; justice is too expensive a thing for the poor man. Offences against the person hardly count for so much as those against property."[258] Inclusion of each other in their lives becomes very necessary.

> To love your neighbor *as* yourself is the whole law and the prophets; to feel that you are "equal" with others, that their lives are as your life, that your life is as theirs—even in what trifling degree we may experience such things—is to enter into another life which includes both sides; it is to pass beyond the sphere of moral distinctions, and to trouble oneself no more with them.[259]

Moral questions were absent in pre-civilisational culture because, for tribals, the tribe was part of their larger life.[260]

Significance for Hind Swaraj/ Gandhian Philosophy: Civilisation as disease, Doctors, health as unity, civilisation as inequality, the separation between mind and body, self and other, not antagonism between human and nature, linking logical and intellectual parts of human beings from the emotional instinct, the law as the morality of ruling classes, inclusion of other in our life.

Thomas F. Taylor

The Fallacy of Speed (1909): Thomas F. Taylor analyses speed vis-à-vis population, profit and pleasure. He notices how time is construed as money, and rapidity is celebrated. But it has its own consequences. "Rapid means of transit accelerate the growth of towns, and by throwing the work of a whole country into the same market, promote competition in unhealthy degrees. The rapid growth of most large industrial centres, which the railway fosters, is in many respects an undesirable one."[261] It also causes slums in towns and an infusion of more population. Speed may act against diversity and heterogeneity.

> We ought to be thankful to-day for differences of language, geographical barrier, and such remaining difficulties of communication as we have in as far as they counteract in a measure needless jostle and competition; allow of an independent growth of customs, arts, and ideas among different peoples; and by keeping the world more or less in compartments, make it both more interesting and more manageable.[262]

The loss of speed can be gained in power in the sphere of poetry and the art of life. Railways accelerate trade. It opens a fresh market. "But this is only half the truth. They bring work to one locality which otherwise would have been done in another and perhaps in healthier fashion."[263] India's main problem of loss of native industries can be cited in this regard. The case of poverty is due to improved communication, which is another aspect. Labour conditions are not good in England, which is "the home and birthplace of the boons and blessings to civilisations".[264] Indian railways are useful to tourists, not to the native population.

Prevention of famine in India due to railways is doubtful due to the depletion of reserved food grain. An extensive system of irrigation should be adopted. Railways does not help to establish a connection between rulers and ruled in India.[265] Speed does not solve the problem of unemployment despite the exploitation of resources by an advanced civilization. "Our advanced civilisation demands a wholesale exploitation of the world's resources; and yet after a century of science and inventions we have still armies of unemployed."[266]

Taylor reminds us speed is interference. "Too often, where the white man meets the black, the liberties of the native are unjustly interfered with. Disturbances are mainly caused by the appropriation of their land, or by some form of taxation-poll-tax or land-tax-to support a government which they don't require."[267] Greater efficiency is not required today. The gospel of speed and high competition block the perception of life on other lines. The condition of factory workers in England has become deplorable. Speed, town, market, competition and productive capacity are intertwined. Towns grow, and the countryside vanishes. Self-contained and evenly balanced country life is conceivable, and its needs can be met locally. Power-driven machinery displaces work from home to factory and country to town, thus the extinction of simpler tools and arts. It is unfortunate that simpler methods are replaced by costly machinery. The wholesale industries uproot home and local industries.[268]

He reasons that in the absence of railways in the past, there was no happy existence. Speed leads to the homogenization of spaces. He hints toward the erosion of "friction" due to rapid communication.[269] "Rapid communications by rail and wire take from our movements the amount of friction that the ideal life seems to require."[270] In the end, he asks the following question: "Does quick locomotion finally tend more to give leisure or to destroy it ?"[271]

Significance for Hind Swaraj/ Gandhian Philosophy: analysis of speed and railway, significance of interdependence, critique of heavy machinery and urbanism. *Indian Opinion* (10 December 1910) carried the piece on speed and its consequences (ઝડપ અને તેનાં માઠાં પરિણામો) in the context of Taylor's contribution in *Indian Opinion* in 1910. This one-page article focuses on the harm caused by machines (particularly railways), the consequences of high speed like overcrowding, and increased harmful contribution.[272]

Godfrey Blount (1859–1937)

A New Crusade: An Appeal (1903): Godfrey Blount protests against materialism. *A New Crusade* urges its readers to live a simple life. It protests useless, cruel and extravagant habits and attempts to correct these. For these, fighting against prevalent materialism and apathy becomes crucial. Materialism entails material acquisition over mental ones, preferring purely intellectual and scientific knowledge over the "unexplainable qualities of spontaneity, imagination and love".[273] For general betterment, the gradual bettering of individuals and fine citizens is an important catalyst for the fine state, not fine laws. Return to country life and handicrafts' over-dependence on machinery and manufacturing towns are recognized desires. It does not appeal for the complete abolition of machinery.[274]

We must begin by discrediting the stereotyped belief that everything must be sacrificed—our health, our peace, our

> agriculture, our peasantry, the beauty of natural scenery,-to the exigencies of competitive mechanical production. It is this popular delusion which directs invention more and more into the elaboration of machinery and a system of production which changes men into slaves and prisoners, and renders their labour automatic.[275]

It appeals to agriculture over factories. The machine is antithetical to peace. Labour exploitation is condemned. Homespun dress is advocated. The power of imagination is possessed by all humans due to inspiration and desire for the world.[276]

Significance for Hind Swaraj/ Gandhian Philosophy: critique of materialism, country life and handicrafts over-dependence on machinery and manufacturing towns, rejection of competitive mechanical production.

Henry David Thoreau (1817–62)

On the Duty of Civil Disobedience (1849): Henry David Thoreau published this pioneering text as resistance to civil government in 1849 (Thoreau, 1849, pp. 189–211). The essay was part of the collection which was done on the high aesthetic ground that is ". . . writers of different schools . . . that shall cultivate an harmonious intellectual and moral life . . . "[277] Thereafter, in a slew of versions, other popular nomenclatures of the essay are "On the Duty of Civil Disobedience" and "Civil Disobedience". In the original essays, long paragraphs are written. The essay was converted into independent books carrying small paragraphs. The text becomes immortal for containing phrases like "That government is best which governs least" and "That government is best which governs not at all."[278] In addition to these two polemical sentences, they contain significant theorisation on civil disobedience, shaping the future discourse on people, state and sovereignty. He does not consider government as an expedient: "Government is at best but an expedient; but most governments are usually, and all governments are sometimes, inexpedient."[279] In him, the criticism against the standing army can be extended to the standing government. "The standing army is only an arm of the standing government."[280] He delinks the majority and conscience concerning deciding right or wrong. "Can there not be a government in which majorities do not virtually decide right and wrong, but conscience?"[281] The human precedes the subject. He chooses "right" over "law". There is an obligation to do a right.[282] Though "a corporation has no conscience; but a corporation of conscientious men is a corporation *with* a conscience."[283] People serve as machines to the state. There are some who serve with conscience and resist, and are thus treated as enemies.[284]

He cites the argument of William Paley's "The Duty of Submission to Civil Government", which was a part of Book VI of *The Principles of Moral Political Philosophy* (1825). For William Paley,

> . . . so long as the interest of the whole society requires it, that is, so long as the established government cannot be resisted or changed without public inconvenience, it is the will of God . . . that the established government be obeyed--and no longer . . . This principle being admitted, the justice of every particular case of resistance is reduced to a computation of the quantity of the danger and grievance on the one side, and of the probability and expense of redressing it on the other.[285]

Thoreau points out that honest people hesitate, regret and petition but do nothing earnestly and effectively.[286] Herein, he draws attention to the idea of obedience or obeying unjust laws. "Unjust laws exist: shall we be content to obey them, or shall we endeavour to amend them, and obey them until we have succeeded, or shall we transgress them at once ?"[287] Since his meeting point of the state through tax collection, he offers to resist it. He places the individual over the state as a higher and independent power, thus urging his readers to treat the theme accordingly.

Significance for Hind Swaraj/ Gandhian Philosophy: Satyagraha, resistance to unjust laws, conscience over the state

Life Without Principle (1863): In this essay, he comes down heavy on business. "I think that there is nothing, not even crime, more opposed to poetry, to philosophy, aye, to life itself, than this incessant *business*."[288] One must get a living by loving. Ordinary conversation has become hollow and reduced to gossip due to life being barred from inward and private space. News is not genius but the stalest repletion.[289] He asks a slew of questions on freedom. "What is it to be free from King George and continue [as] the slaves of King Prejudice? What is it to be born free and not to live free? What is the value of any political freedom but as a means to moral freedom? Is it a freedom to be slaves, or a freedom to be free, of which we boast?"[290] He also touches upon the question of representation. "There is a part of us which is not represented. It is taxation without representation. We quarter troops, we quarter fools and cattle of all sorts upon ourselves."[291] The essay concludes with two metaphorical uses of eupeptics and dyspeptics, prioritizing positive over painful. "Why should we not meet, not always as dyspeptics, to tell our bad dreams, but sometimes as eupeptics, to congratulate each other on the ever-glorious morning."[292]

Significance for Hind Swaraj/ Gandhian Philosophy: Ethical life, moral freedom

John Ruskin (1819–1900)

Unto this Last (1862): John Ruskin's book addresses "The Roots of Honor", "The Vein of Wealth", "Qui Judicates Terram" and "Ad Valorem". In the preface, he suggests establishing training schools at government cost throughout the country. Children should be taught with the best skilful teaching. Then, three things could be produced: (1) (a) the laws of health, and the exercises enjoined by them; (b) habits of gentleness and justice and (c) the calling by which he is to live;[293] (2) establishment of manufactories and workshops under government regulation; (3) work for unemployed men, women, boys and girls who once received government school education at the nearest on fixed wages.[294] He expands the idea of political economy for the contribution of all. In the political economy of state or citizens and its scope, famer, builder, housewife, singer ". . . are all political economists in the true and final sense; adding continually to the riches and well-being of the nation to which they belong".[295] In contrast to it, ". . . But mercantile economy, the economy of 'merces' or of 'pay', signifies the accumulation, in the hands of individuals, of legal or moral claim upon, or power over, the labour of others; every such claim implying precisely as much poverty or debt on one side, as it implies riches or right on the other."[296] There is almost not much ". . . addition to the actual property, or well-being of the State in which it exists".[297]

He rejects inequality as an advantageous proposition. It is unjustly established and causes injury to the nation.[298] Commercial tax cannot be the component to the principle of economy. The commercial tax is "[b]uy in the cheapest market and sell in the dearest."[299] "The money power is always imperfect and doubtful; there are many things which cannot be reached with it, others which cannot be retained by it. Many joys may be given to men which cannot be bought for gold . . . "[300] He makes clear the difference between what is legal and what is just. "For it is possible among certain nations, or under certain rulers, or by the help of certain advocates, that proceedings may be legal which are by no means just."[301] *Ad Valorem* is "To be 'valuable', therefore, is to 'avail towards life.'"[302]

In the backdrop of the assertion of self-interest in political economy, Ruskin prefers life over wealth.

> THERE IS NO WEALTH BUT LIFE. Life, including all its powers of love, of joy, and of admiration. That country is the richest which nourishes the greatest number of noble and happy human beings; that man is richest who, having perfected the functions of his own life to the utmost, has also the widest helpful influence, both personal and by means of his possessions, over the lives of others.[303]

Moreover, "[t]he rich not only refuse food to the poor; they refuse wisdom; they refuse virtue; they refuse salvation."[304] There should be universalization of luxury. It cannot be reduced to a few. "Luxury is indeed possible in the future—innocent and exquisite; luxury for all, and by the help of all; but luxury at present can only be enjoyed by the ignorant . . . "[305]

Significance for Hind Swaraj/ Gandhian Philosophy: Gandhi translated *Unto This Last* as *Sarvodaya* in Gujarati. He summarizes the teaching of the book into three axioms:

> 1. That the good of the individual is contained in the good of all. 2. That a lawyer's work has the same value as the barber's in as much as all have the same right of earning their livelihood from their work. 3. That a life of labour, i.e., the life of the tiller of the soil and the handicraftsman is the life worth living.[306]

He knew the first principle and realised dimly the second one. And the third one alluded to him. "*Unto This Last* made it as clear as daylight for me that the second and the third were contained in the first. I arose with the dawn, ready to reduce these principles to practice."[307]

A Joy for Ever (And Its Price in the Market) (1857): John Ruskin's two lectures ("The Discovery and Application of Art", a lecture delivered at Manchester, 10 July 1857) and "The Accumulation and Distribution of Art" (continuation of the previous lecture, delivered 13 July 1857) constitute this book. The first page of the book contains John Keats's famous poem "Endymion's" first line: "A thing of beauty is a joy forever." According to Keats, "A thing of beauty is a joy forever: Its loveliness increases; it will never Pass into nothingness . . . "[308] The beauty of a work of art has both "honoured permanence" and local influence.[309] Against this backdrop, he touches on the economy and labour. All economy is nothing but managing labour or wise management of labour (applying labour rationally, reserving produce carefully and distributing produce seasonally).[310] He cautions against unnecessary expenditure. He compares the work of "true goldsmith's work . . . [as] . . . the means of education of the greatest painters and sculptors of the day".[311]

Our consumption is linked with the labour of people who are compelled to produce certain articles.[312] It is important to note that "[w]herever you go, whatever you do, act more for *preservation* and less for *production*."[313] No good work was ever done for money.[314] He also invites attention to the nature of action and subsequent implications.

> All enmity, jealousy, opposition, and secrecy are wholly and in all circumstances, destructive in their nature—not productive; and all kindness, fellowship, and communicativeness are invariably productive in their operation—not destructive: and the evil principles of opposition and exclusiveness are not rendered less fatal, but more fatal, by their acceptance among large masses of men; more fatal, I say, exactly in proportion as their influence is more secret.[315]

He also suggests the different outcomes of "wealth ill-used" and "wealth well used": "wealth ill-used was as the net of the spider, entangling and destroying: but wealth well used is as the net of the sacred fisher who gathers souls of men out of the deep."[316]

Significance for Hind Swaraj/ Gandhian Philosophy: Ethical action, morality over money, meaningfulness in wealth use

Giuseppe Mazzini (1805–72)

Duties of Men (1862): Giuseppe Mazzini, in his "Preface to the Italian Working Class" in this book, invites attention to certain principles. This is the progress of the country along with the emancipation of this class. His republication instincts emphasize the true man, not the rich or great man. A great democratic unity cannot be based on aristocracy and monarchy. There is equality and sharing through association. He calls Machiavellism and materialism two sores. The first leads to dishonesty and the second to egotism and anarchy through it, the idea of worshipping interest.[317] Capital in a few hands leads to want and poverty of a multitude. Hours of labour and more remuneration are needed. "Men of duty" focuses on the others, whereas "the men of rights" focuses on the self and the labour of the other. The theory of rights contrasts with the common good. Any order based on violence is a tyranny. The theory of right may overthrow tyranny but cannot establish harmony among various elements of the nation. Living for the other is vital.[318] Each human ". . . is bound to live, not for himself, but for others . . . "[319] Moreover, ". . . struggle against injustice and error, wherever they exist, in the name and for the benefit of their brothers, is not only a *right* but a Duty:— a duty which may not be neglected without sin:—the duty of whole life."[320] There can be rights only when duties are enshrined that is common good.[321]

His comments are scathing on "governing laws". "You have no rights of citizenship, nor participation—either of election or vote—in those laws which are to direct your actions and govern your life. How can you feel the sentiment of citizenship, zeal for the State, or sincere affection for its laws?"[322] In addition, "[y]our poverty frequently involves the impossibility of your obtaining justice like other classes."[323] Righteousness of means is essential. The wealthier classes know the suffering of the poor but do not feel it.[324] ". . . [T]he kingdom of God *on Earth* as it is in Heaven or rather, that Earth may become a preparation for Heaven, and society and endeavour after the progressive realisation of the Divine Idea."[325]

On the one hand, preaching virtue, sacrifice and love are essential, and on the other hand, speaking thoughts bodily and making wants courageously without anger and reaction are equally necessary. Earth is for improvement and development towards a higher stage of existence. God has not created to contemplate but to act. Life is governed by a higher law. Conscience is a crucial factor. Individual conscience and the common consent of humanity are both sacred. Not interrogating either one is not reaching the truth. Duties are to be positive. Action is vital. Being is humanity. Education is crucial to knowing the duties that are first geared towards humanity. The medium of association is necessary for rational, social and intellectual progress.[326] "Wheresoever a man is tortured through error, injustice or tyranny, that man is your brother. Free men or slaves, you are all brothers."[327] Association and cooperation are essential for a common aim. While making God the central actor, he expands the maxim or norms under the "unity" principle. "The true Country is a Community of free men and equals, bound together in fraternal concord to labour towards a common aim . . . the Country is not an *aggregation*, but an *association*."[328] A true country must have universal rights.[329]

The law should be universal in a substantive sense. "The Laws should be the expression of the *universal* aspiration and promote the universal good. They should be a pulsation of the heart of the Nation. The entire Nation should, either directly or indirectly, legislate."[330] It cannot be reduced to a few hands. "Country is not a mere some zone of territory. The true Country is the Idea to which it gives birth; it is the Thought of Love, the sense of communion which unites in one all the sons of that territory."[331] Without participation in the development of national life, education for all and work for all, ". . . you have no Country in the sense in which Country ought to exist, the Country of all and for all."[332] The three pillars of the nation are education, labour and the franchise. Sacrifice for humanity will make life in the country immortal.[333]

Women are the core of the country.[334] "Cancel from your minds every idea of superiority over woman. You have none whatsoever. Long prejudice, an inferior education, and a perennial legal inequality and injustice have created that *apparent* intellectual inferiority which has been converted into an argument of continued oppression."[335] There are no men and women, and they must not be unequal.[336] Women must be considered partners, companions and equals in civil and political life.[337] The law of life is progress for individuals and humanity.[338] Sovereignty lies not with the individual but with the nation, humanity and society. There cannot be command without consent. The majority cannot decree tyranny or alienate its own freedom.[339] Liberty is indispensable for the moral and material components of life— personal liberty, liberty of locomotion, liberty of religious faith; liberty of opinion, liberty of expressions through press or other peaceful means; liberty of associations; liberty of labour, trade, commerce and produce are not to be denied without right to protest.[340] "The Press must be absolutely free. The rights of intellect are inviolable, and every *preventive* censorship is tyranny."[341] The right to peaceful association is sacred.[342] Education is crucial. Education addresses moral faculty, whereas instruction is to the intellectual domain. Education ". . . develops in man the knowledge of his duties; the second gives him the capacity of achieving them. Without instruction, education would be too often inefficient; without education, instruction is a lever deprived of its fulcrum."[343] Everyone is entitled to be heard and should be encouraged.[344] People are interpreted as law.[345] He rejects the principle of self-interest and each for himself in political economy. The emancipation of women and working men are intertwined in arriving at the universal truth.[346]

Significance for Hind Swaraj/ Gandhian Philosophy: true man, democratic unity, capital as want and poverty of multitude, common good, rejection of violence, problematizing governing laws, people as sovereign, earth as heaven, preaching virtue-sacrifice-love, higher stage of existence, life by higher law, association, womens' rights.

Plato (427—347 BCE)

Defence and Death of Socrates: Plato's *Apology, Euthyphro, Crito and Phaedo* are related to the trial and death of Socrates.[347] Amidst a slew of translations, "Gandhi does not say which translation of Plato he read in jail, in 1908, but he is likely to have read the *Defence and Death of Socrates*, which was a small book that contained only the *Apology* and part of the *Phaedo* in [Henry] Cary's translation."[348] Henry Francis Cary's work (*The Defence and Death of Socrates; Being the "Apology" and Parts of the "Phaedo;" or "The Immortality of the Soul" of Plato*, London: Arthur C. Fifield) was published in 1905. Socrates, a seventy-year-old, was tried in the spring of 399 BCE for impiety and corrupting youth. Meletus was the chief accuser, seconded by Anytus ("bitter enemy of sophists") and Lyco (an aristocrat or a person of no significance). Socrates's criticism of poets incensed him. A court of 501 tried Socrates. The debate continues whether Socrates delivered the speech or if it was Plato's imagination. Though less charming, it is considered his speech than his present finished form. The Athenian Court voted for Socrates' condemnation. Despite not being a sophist, his condemnation was considered prevalent hostility towards sophists. He was not teaching for payment or promising a definite outcome. He also did not investigate the natural phenomenon or promise financial gain to hearers. His aims were the path to righteousness and becoming perfect individuals. It looked harmless. The path to righteousness is also based on making people think. Thinking about religion was not liked by conservatives. Conversion between sophists and Socrates through "thought" augmented suspicion and hostility towards the latter. His *Daimonion* (inner voice) was considered to reject the state's gods.[349]

He asserts his saying at his trial as just.[350] Upon being declared the wisest man by the oracle at Delphi, he examines people who are more intelligent or wise than him. After examining the person who was a public figure, his observation became very pertinent.

> . . . [T]his man seemed to me to seem to be wise to many other people and especially to himself, but not to be so; and then I tried to show him that he thought he was wise, but was not. As a result, I became hateful to him and to many of those present; and so, as I went away, I thought to myself, "I am wiser than this man; for neither of us really knows anything fine and good, but this man thinks he knows something when he does not, whereas I, as I do not know anything, do not think I do either. I seem, then, in just this little thing to be wiser than this man at any rate, that what I do not know I do not think I know either."[351]

Socrates highlights the importance of being critiqued, which is needed to wake the consciousness of society.

> For if you put me to death, you will not easily find another, who, to use a rather absurd figure, attaches himself to the city as a gadfly to a horse, which, though large and well bred, is sluggish

on account of his size and needs to be aroused by stinging. I think the Gods fastened me upon the city in some such capacity, and I go about arousing, and urging and reproaching each one of you, constantly alighting upon you everywhere the whole day long. Such another is not likely to come to you, gentlemen; but if you take my advice, you will spare me.[352]

He cautions against his killing for such a cause.

But you, perhaps, might be angry, like people awakened from a nap, and might slap me, as Anytus advises, and easily kill me; then you would pass the rest of your lives in slumber, unless God, in his care for you, should send someone else to sting you. And that I am, as I say, a kind of gift from the god, you might understand from this; for I have neglected all my own affairs and have been enduring the neglect of my concerns all these years, but I am always busy in your interest, coming to each one of you individually like a father or an elder brother and urging you to care for virtue.[353]

Significance for Hind Swaraj/ Gandhian Philosophy: Gandhi paraphrased and published Plato's *Apology* as *Ek Satyavirni Katha* (Story of A Soldier of Truth) in six issues of the *Indian Opinion*. The preface of *Story of A Soldier of Truth* was published on 4 April 1908. Socrates is morally excellent, virtuous and a reformer who is devoid of fear of death. He calls for a fight against corrupt elements or the observation of traditional religion. For this, Socrates was condemned to death by poisoning. He exhibited no sign of fear. He provides learning to live and die. He is a great satyagrahi because he uses satyagraha against his own people. Socrates becomes imperative to fight against the disease that is the oppression by the British regime.[354] Knowing the true state of ignorance;[355] examining Meletus;[356] the problem of judgment by the majority, importance of the right act, fearlessness from death, importance of means over money, importance of the soul, wisdom and truth over honour and reputation, striving for perfection, virtue causes wealth not otherwise;[357] dying for the chosen path, need of a critique, critiquing majoritarianism, justice as a central category, no fear of death, no appealing;[358] final speech before death, adherence to integrity, appeal to the extension of his principles to his sons before people.[359]

Max Nordau (1849–1923)

Conventional Lies of Our Civilization (1883): Gandhi mentions "Paradoxes of Civilisation" by Max Nordau. This is an admixture of his two books. *The Conventional Lies of Civilization* (1883) and *Paradox* (1886) are two separate books. *The Conventional Lies of Civilization* is a powerful indictment of civilization discourse. Besides the preface (or prefaces), the book is organized into "Mene, Tekel, Upharsin", "The Lie of Religion", "The Lie of a Monarchy and Aristocracy", "The Political Lie", "The Economic Lie" and "the Matrimonial Lie". According to him, ". . . that the present social, political and economic institutions are utterly at variance with the views and conceptions of the universe based upon natural science, and therefore untenable and doomed to destruction".[360] Against the backdrop of the book ban by the Imperial Council of Vienna on the grounds of crime inflicted against religion, public peace and imperial family, he avers that his analyses are not targeted against individuals but ideas. In the backdrop of the analysis of the Russian state, the gap between the state and mutual rights and public officials versus the country's interest, people and misuse of laws are highlighted.[361] He criticizes the confluence of the Church and the aristocracy of rank and wealth. This is the promotion of each other's interests. Two distinct developments are visible: submission of middle classes to the written and unwritten laws of dominant classes; exclusion of labourers and laws of dominant classes (he used 'dominant castes'); exclusion of labourers and the tenants outside of capital and land. Reading from the lens of the English working man was crucial rather than a tea grounds perspective to understand the future of England, which was dark and threatening.[362] He also alludes to "pessimism" as a method for understanding philosophical thought, inquiry and important problems of the day.[363] "Pessimism has a physiological basis, and a certain measure of suffering is entailed upon us by the nature of our organism. It is by suffering that we first become conscious of our Ego."[364] Unlike the French Revolution, pessimism in his time, ". . . lowers like a dense, black cloud over the vast majority of cultivated human beings".[365]

Inequality and hierarchy become a part of a civilization. ". . . [W]e are obliged to live in the midst of a civilization, which allows one man, by the accident of his birth, to assume the most extensive rights over millions of his fellow-men, his equals in every respect and in many cases, his superiors."[366] The lie becomes a core element in his analysis. "Every word that we speak, every action, is a direct lie against that which we acknowledge as truth in our hearts."[367] He attempts to unravel the "discordant strife between the principal conventional lies of our civilization, and the truths they deny, based on natural science, which we have adopted as our conceptions of the universe".[368] In place of religion as "supernatural power and abstract powers", he calls religion as practice "a conventional lie of civilized society" and "a functional weakness".[369] This came after his pondering over religion as causality and treatment of being as "anthropomorphite",[370] causing the non-existence of the Ego.[371] Poetry, music, art, thought and humanity were crucial for the fuller life of the community[372] against the religious ceremony.[373] The state remains complicit in the extension of imposition of religion by declaring or allocating certain days for performance.[374]

He combines religion and monarchy to ensure each other's existence.[375] Herein, command and being commanded, and thereafter, the role of religion is highlighted. The reasoning of the average citizens is as follows: "You are a human being like the rest of us; as we did not appoint you voluntarily to be a ruler over us, we are surely not bound to pay homage to you and obey your commands."[376] The reply of the tyrant is as follows: "Your argument is indisputable, but so is my army. You will obey my commands not because they are rational and convincing, but because I will compel you to do so."[377] The aegis of religion becomes crucial for maintaining legitimacy after death.[378] People's sovereignty annuls the monarchy. "Viewed from the standpoint of the sovereign people, the constitutional monarchy appears fully as unreasonable."[379] The use and abuse of religion by Monarchy is widespread in the book. He does not see the hope and possibility of a republic amidst such a civilization.[380]

Nordau redefines a republic as the realization of self-government in which supreme authority lies with the people. "A republic is the last link of a long chain of development. It is the form of government in which the ideal of self-government finds realization—the supreme power residing ultimately in the whole people and directly exercised by them."[381] Changing the government with unchanged structures makes little sense.

"An exclusively political revolution, changing merely the form of the government from monarchical to republican, and leaving undisturbed the existing conditions of society, philosophy and economy, of which the monarchy is the logical sequence, has neither sense nor foundation."[382] He does not give much significance to a theocratic state, even of a republican nature. He contests that sovereignty derives from divine sources.[383] He needs to see the possibility of the Parliament's catalytic impact on government. ". . . [T]he Parliament has no authority or influence to change any of the decisions of the Government."[384] His model resides in the most enlightened person.[385] However, his aristocracy is not hereditary due to the violation of individual rights and nepotism. His aristocracy comprises highly qualified humans or the best and noblest person.[386]

The political lie is associated with the evaluation of the nature of the state. "The State as at present organized, is a machine which works with an enormous waste of power."[387] He also calls anarchy an incapability of correct observation. Citizens are made the property of the sovereign. Officials use the laws to defend the master. He dubs Parliamentism as a lie due to unchanging of the internal organization of the state. Representative legislation is machinery wherefrom people exercise their sovereignty. Eventually, due to the constantly increasing size of the state, the direct practice of self-government becomes an impossibility. It leads to the envisioning of rule by small numbers through delegation.[388] "The seats in the legislative assembly must not be filled by men, but by mandates, who speak and vote."[389] Despite the introduction of representative legislation, people ". . . are ruled by an individual will and they are plundered by a privileged class; only this will is no longer called the king, but the leader of his party and the privileged class, not the aristocracy, but the majority in the House. The old relation between the average citizen and the State remains unaltered . . . "[390] Citizens as minority and majority with professional politicians become stark in his analysis. ". . . [T] he citizen who conscientiously tries to practise his political rights with a view to the welfare of the community, will always find himself in the minority, while the majority are following the lead of the professional politicians who carry on their public life as a regular lucrative business career."[391]

Eloquence is extremely important in parliament. "The most important ally of the will in Parliament, is eloquence."[392] "But only in the rarest cases has a debate led to any really important parliamentary resolution."[393] Theoretical division and practical applicability become categorical. "The forces which theoretically keep the parliamentary machine in motion, are experience, foresight and abnegation of self; in reality they are strength of will, egotism and fluency of speech."[394]

The economic lie suggests the existence of a massive contrast between the rich and the poor. The alternative lies in agriculture. "As long as a people are only familiar with agriculture, cattle-raising and domestic industries, although they may be poor in money and articles of luxury, yet the necessaries of life are within the reach of every individual."[395] Free tillers are crucial for being free from the poor. Absolute poverty, as well as cities and manufacturing industries, are identified as core concerns.

A highly developed civilization thus condemns a group of individuals increasing daily in numbers and importance, to absolute poverty. The cities grow at the expense of the farming population. It favours the great manufacturing industries at the expense of animal and vegetable production, and produces a

numerous-wages receiving class, whose members cannot call
a single inch of ground their own and live under abnormal
conditions of existence, condemned to slow starvation the day
that their factory, work-room or dock yard is closed.[396]

The only liberty that labour has is the liberty of dying of hunger
or maintaining a bare existence or overwork and starvation.[397]
The iron law of wages is an infamous lie. "The statistics of the
records of disease and death among the laboring classes of
Europe, brand the 'iron law of wages' as an infamous lie."[398]
Speculation in the economy makes the economy a bad domain,
along with the appropriation of wealth. "We have thus seen that
great wealth in almost all cases, is due to the appropriation of the
results of others' labor, not one's own."[399] Milliners are backed
by laws and religion.[400]

The political economy of our civilization presents a painful
division of accumulation and subsistence economy.

Our picture of the political economy of our civilization in
the preceding pages, included the privileged class, the men of
wealth and leisure, who live on the labor of others, the group
of college-bred young men who consider that their possession
of a diploma entitles them to live the life of a parasite on the
working classes, the same as the millionaire's wealth entitles
him, and the *proletaires*, the lowest class in society, torn from
the soil intended by nature to support man, without property
of any kind, toiling for a mere subsistence.[401]

In fact, in place of offering liberty and prosperity, civilization
excludes day labourers from partaking.[402] Therefore, "[t]he great
end and aim of humanity in the field of political economy, is

not the production of commodities for which a price can be obtained, but to satisfy with its labor the actual organic wants of the body."[403] He proposes that "[t]he right of inheritance must be abolished."[404]

Matrimonial lies are concerned with the reduction of love in marriage and the arrival of capitalist contracts for profit.[405] "In society marriages are not entered into on account of love, but to obtain rank and wealth."[406] He laments the reduction of marriage as women's only career and destiny.[407] The right to divorce and education for girls is crucial to him.[408]

Significance for Hind Swaraj/Gandhian Philosophy: Powerful indictment of civilization discourse, critique of organized religion, inequality, critique of the state, republic as the realization of self-government, sovereignty with people not in divine power, critique of parliamentarism.

Paradoxes (1886): This is an engaging text in which Max Nordau highlights many paradoxes. According to Nordau, the chief aim of the *Paradoxes* ". . . is to demonstrate that even what is most self-evident is still open to many doubts and may lead to much perplexity, as it frequently happens that the same fact may be supported by the most opposite theories and explanation, which all seem equally plausible and probably are all equally erroneous".[409] The book deals with optimism and pessimism, majority and minority, retrospect, success, the psycho-physiological of genius and talent, suggestion, gratitude, the importance of fiction, the natural history of love, evolution in aesthetics, symmetry, generalization, where is truth, the state as an annihilator of character, nationality and a glance into the future. In addition to other contributions, the book poses paradoxes concerning the formulation of majority and minority. He highlights the phenomenon of despising the masses and taking the decision or legitimacy in their name. "On the one hand, we assert that we despise the masses, on the other hand all that we do is done with them in view. We refuse to believe the masses capable of passing judgement upon the productions of genius, and yet the fairest dream of genius is fame and immortality, that is, appreciation of by the masses."[410] The masses' lack of intelligence and legitimacy are significant paradoxes.

> We deny that the masses have intelligence, and yet representative legislation, trial by jury, and public opinion, all institutions regarded with the utmost respect, are founded upon the assumption that the majority is not only supreme in its wisdom but even perfectly infallible. We look upon being classed with the masses as a degradation, and yet on all momentous occasions we are proud to feel and think with the crowd.[411]

Significance for Hind Swaraj/ Gandhian Philosophy: the rejection of the superficial notion of majority and minority;

Dadabhai Naoroji (1825–1917)

Poverty and Un-British Rule in India: Dadabhai Naoroji published *Poverty and India: Papers and Statistics* in 1888. It contains papers read before the Bombay Branch of the East India Company in 1876. In it, he highlights the suffering and sinking in poverty of India under the present system of administration.[412] Excessive drain of wealth and poverty in India and excessive employment of Europeans are correlated. It put the British government into a false moral position.[413] The drain of India's wealth and excessive expenditure of the state led ". . . the rulers to all sorts of ingenious and oppressive devices to make the two ends meet , and to descend more and more every day to the principles of Asiatic despotism , so contrary to English grain and genius".[414] "All salaries and pensions . . . paid to Europeans in England and India . . . are actually . . . a direct deprivation of the natural provision for similar classes of the people of the country, and . . . a drain from the property and capacity of the country at large."[415] He insists on stopping the "bleeding drain" from India. "I repeat, therefore, with every earnestness, that the most important question of the day is, how to stop the bleeding drain from India."[416] *Poverty and Un-British Rule in India* was published in 1901. The introduction was added to the 1888 edition in which "Un-British Rule" became the reference point of analysis. "The title of the book is 'POVERTY AND UN-BRITISH RULE IN INDIA', i.e., the present system of government is destructive and despotic to the Indians and un-British and suicidal to Britain. On the other hand, a truly British course can and will certainly be vastly beneficent both to Britain and India."[417] A slew of benefits are as follows: abolition of *sati* and infanticide; introduction of English education and thus introduction of the highest political ideal of British citizenship; Act of 1833 and the Queen's Proclamations of 1858, 1877 and 1887; improvement of law and order.[418] A slew of the features of the un-British system are as follows: bleeding drain over £30,000,000 a year; war cost imposed on India; expenditure of British interest charged to India; no voice in expenditure of the revenue; the power of government as arbitrary, despotic, alien and bleeding.[419]

Significance for Hind Swaraj/ Gandhian Philosophy: critique of railway, critique of colonization and the rejection of capitalism/ imperialism; pauperization due to lack of attention; stress on agriculture;

Romesh Chunder Dutt (1848–1909)

Economic History of India: Romesh Chunder Dutt wrote the *Economic History of India* in two volumes published in 1902 and 1904. The preface to the first edition of volume one briefly touches on the positive and negative contributions of the British administration while highlighting the absence of the history of the people of India, trade, industry and agriculture. According to Dutt, conferring peace, western education, modern thought, modern sciences, modern institutions and life are significant contributions made by Englishmen to India. However, poverty and famine are two developments unexampled in the nineteenth century of India.

> By a moderate calculation the famines of 1877 and 1878, of 1889 and 1892, of 1897 and 1900, have carried off fifteen millions of people. The population of a fair-sized European country has been swept away from India within twenty-five years. A population equal to half of that of England has perished in India within a period.[420]

Unravelling the actual cause of "Indian poverty" and "Indian famine" became the utmost priority. The production of cultivators under pressure from moneylenders under the government revenue demand, the selfish commercial policy of the East India Company and the British Parliament for discouraging Indian manufacturers to encourage manufacturing in England, supply of raw material from India, forcing Indians to work in Company's factories, the invention of the power loom in England, excise duty on production of cotton fabrics, excessive land tax, appropriation of incomes and gains of tillers, no fostering of new industries, increasing revenue causing more destitution, depositing of profit in Europe were crucial factors for Indian poverty and Indian famines.[421] The East India Company and Indian debt were crucial factors. "The East India Company's trade was abolished in 1833, and the Company was abolished in 1858, but their policy remains. Their capital was paid off by loans which were made into an Indian debt, on which interest is paid from Indian taxes."[422] Wealth creation and taxes remitted out of the country were worrisome developments. People were denied representation by the Indian government.[423] On this, Dutt offers scathing criticism. "History does not record a single instance of one people ruling another in the interests of the subject nation."[424]

> In each Indian District again, there is a District Board, and Village Unions are being formed. These Unions are the modern counterparts of those ancient Village Communities which have been described repeatedly in the following pages, and which were self-governing little republics all over India under Hindu and Mahomedan governments. They have been swept away, somewhat hastily and unwisely, under British rule.[425]

He points out the failure of bringing the two reforms during the reign of Queen Victoria:

> It has not admitted the people of India to any share in the control and direction of the administration of their own affairs. And it has not improved the material condition of the mass of the people, or protected the country from those frequent, fatal, and widespread famines which have now disappeared from all other lands under civilised administrations.[426]

He reminds his readers that "it is impossible to govern a country in the interests of the people without bestowing on that people some degree of self-government and representation."[427]

Dutt also highlights the income gulf between India and other parts of the Empire. "In Canada and other Colonies, the income per head of the population is £48 per year. In Great Britain, it is £42. In India it is officially estimated at £2."[428] Public debt was a perennial concern for him. Poverty added to the severity of famines. Growing cotton for the British handloom became a pressing concern over the improvement of Indian handlooms. Taxes sent outside the country are lost forever. The construction of railways by guaranteed companies played a significant role in it. "Between 1877 and 1900, the Public Debt rose from 139 millions to 224 millions. This was largely due to the construction of railways by Guaranteed Companies or by the State, beyond the pressing needs of India and beyond her resources."[429] In addition, the Afghan wars (1878 and 1897) also played a significant role. Irrigation must be given priority over railways. "All further extension of railways from State loans, or under guarantee of interest from the taxes, should be prohibited. Irrigation work should be extended, as far as possible, from the ordinary revenues. The annual Economic Drain from India should be steadily reduced . . . "[430]

The British policies on railways and irrigation complicated the Indian misery.

There was no "cessation of heavy outlay" on the construction of railways. There was no "suspension" of new railway schemes and works. "The first place" among famine-prevention works was not assigned to irrigation.

The reasons, are that the Indian administration is very considerably influenced by the trend of public opinion in England, and not by the opinion of the people of India. Englishmen understand railways, and do not understand the importance of irrigation for India.[431]

The role of members of Parliament became crucial. "Members of Parliament urged the construction of new railway lines by frequent questions in the House of Commons. None cares for irrigation because none in England understands its supreme importance for India."[432] Accordingly, "[n]ew railway lines were pushed on vigorously beyond the urgent needs of India, and certainly beyond her resources."[433] Dutt states that "[w]hen we turn from railways to the subject of irrigation works we turn from unwise extravagance to equally unwise niggardliness."[434] For Dutt, "[d]uring half a century numerous works have been constructed which the country did not urgently need, and many works have been neglected which were vital to the protection of agriculture."[435] The British Empire should be remembered as the giver of peace but not prosperity.

Significance for Hind Swaraj/ Gandhian Philosophy: the rejection of capitalism/imperialism; pauperization due to lack of attention; stress on agriculture;

Henry Sumner Maine (1822–88)

Village-communities in the East and West (1871): Henry Sumner Maine authored this book to highlight comparative jurisprudence. Six lectures constitute the substance of his arguments in the book. His three lectures were added in subsequent editions and delivered as vice-chancellor of the University of Calcutta. In addition to

custom and family (patriarchal family as a unit), he invites attention
to village communities in India and its parallel equivalence in
the West. "The Village-Community is in India itself the source
of a land-law which, in bulk, at all events, may be not unfairly
compared with the real-property law of England."[436] According
to Maine, codified law in India is theoretically connected by a
certain sacerdotal nature. "But the most recent observation goes
to prove that the portion of the law codified and the influence
of this law are much less than was once supposed, and that large
bodies of indigenous custom have grown up independently of the
codified law."[437] Maine acknowledges the presence and effect of
the Brahminical theory of caste and offers a different reasoning.
"The true view of India is that, as a whole, it is divided into a vast
number of independent, self-acting, organised social groups—
trading, manufacturing, cultivating."[438] This is because ". . .
the smaller organic groups of Indian society are very differently
situated."[439] Maine outlines the significance of customary laws
over codified laws.

> Such a system in the end beats all but the experts; and
> we, accordingly, have turned our laws over to experts,
> to attorneys and solicitors, to barristers above them,
> and to judges in the last resort. There is but one remedy
> for this—the reduction of the law to continuous
> writing and its inclusion within aptly-framed general
> propositions. The facilitation of this process is the
> practical end of scientific jurisprudence.[440]

He pays attention specifically to the law. Law is a command from
the political superior/sovereign that addresses political inferiors/

subjects to impose obligation or duty and penalty/sanction in case of disobedience.

> The power vested in particular members of the community of drawing down the sanction on neglects or breaches of the duty is called a Right. Now, without the most violent forcing of language, it is impossible to apply these terms, *command, sovereign, obligation, sanction, right*, to the customary law under which the Indian village-communities have lived for centuries, practically knowing no other law civilly obligatory.[441]

Moreover, customary law is not operated by sanctions. Despite innumerable tenantry, the commons were a peculiar feature. The Eastern and Western villages are combined through identical village communities. "It does not appear to me a hazardous proposition that the Indian and the ancient European systems of enjoyment and tillage by men grouped in village-communities are in all essential particulars identical."[442] Moreover, "the customary rules securing the interdependence and mutual responsibility of the members of an Indian village-community . . . appear to be worthy of careful examination."[443] He refers to a person's village council as a representative body not constituted by inherent authority.[444] He rules out Indian people as military people. Organized and self-acting are another feature of the Indian cultivating groups and the primitive Western communities.[445] "Sometimes the community is unconnected with any exterior body, save by the shadowy bond of caste . . . But in all cases the community is so organised as to be complete in itself."[446]

Significance for Hind Swaraj/ Gandhian Philosophy: village communities, codified laws, customary laws, self-organised groups, commons

Epistemic Significance for Gandhi's Heterodoxy

In addition to other significant sources, Gandhi's heterodoxy borrows significantly from reading these twenty-one books. In heterodoxy, the principles of reconciliation and antagonism are crucial components.

Some of the critical and significant components of the principle of reconciliation based on these twenty books are as follows: *non-violence; symmetry between means and ends; truth, morality, East and West synthesis; fellow feelings; dialogical self; acting as to conscience of truth, multi-religious pluralism, feelings for workers, health as unity, linking self and other; reconciliation between human and nature; linking logical and intellectual parts of human beings from the emotional instinct; inclusion of other in our life; intertwined local relationship; country life and handicrafts; conscientious individuals; ethical life; moral freedom; sound of the individual as the good of all; equal value of all work; valuable life of labour; ethical action; meaningfulness in wealth use; true man; democratic unity; common good; people as sovereign; earth as heaven; preaching virtue- sacrifice-love; higher stage of existence, life by higher law; association; womens' rights; Individuals as morally excellent; virtuous, reformer and devoid of fear of death; learning to live and die; importance of means over money; importance of soul, wisdom and truth over honour and reputation; striving for perfection; wealth arises from virtue, not the other way around; importance of right action; sovereignty with people not in divine power; republic as the realization of self-government; People as non-minority or majority category; people need non-discriminatory treatment; village communities, customary laws, self-organised groups, commons.*

The principle of antagonism is as follows: *Act for swaraj against unjust structures; recognition of labour in form of bread labour;*

rejection of the empiricist notion of pleasure; pursuance of higher law against lower law; conscience over majoritarianism; conscience against the majoritarianism led ethos based Parliament; rejection of violence; preferring soul force against brute forces; controlling palate and rejection of consumption driven being; abstinence from animal food thus preferring vegetarianism and fasting; plight of working people linked to consumption of affluent classes; against exploiting workers and the working class; refusal to participate in violence; satyagraha, disobedience against tyranny; not eye for an eye; modern civilization as a site of violence; non-participation in evil or injustice; indictment of modern civilization for vulnerable condition of male and female workers; civilization as disease; fault lines concerning doctors; civilization as inequality; against the separation between mind and body; law as the morality of ruling classes; analysis of speed and railway; significance of interdependence; critique of heavy machinery and urbanism; critique of materialism; rejection of over dependence on machinery and manufacturing towns; rejection of competitive mechanical production; satyagraha, resistance to unjust laws; conscience over the state; putting idea of equality and equal worthiness into practice against the unjust structures; rejection of money over morality; capital as want and poverty of multitude; problematizing governing laws; fight against the corrupt element or observation of the traditional religion; Satyagrahi/satyagraha against disease that is the oppression by the British Regime; problem of judgment by majority; die for the chosen path; need of a critique, critiquing majoritarianism; justice as a central category, no fear of death, no appealing; critique of civilization discourse; critique of organized religion; critique of inequality, the state; critique of parliamentarism; the rejection of the superficial notion of majority and minority; critique of railway; critique of colonization and the rejection of capitalism/imperialism;

against pauperization; stress on agriculture the rejection of capitalism/ imperialism; pauperization due to lack of attention; stress on agriculture; rejection of Railway centric development; problematic of codified laws.

Sr. No.	Books	Gandhi's Heterodoxy	
		Principle of Reconciliation	Principle of Antagonism
		Leo Tolstoy	
1	*The Kingdom of God is Within You* (1894)	Non-violence, symmetry between means and ends, truth, morality, East and West synthesis	Act for swaraj against unjust structures; recognition of labour in the form of bread labour
2	*What is Art?*(1904)	Fellow feelings, moving away from the empiricist notion of pleasure	Rejection of the empiricist notion of pleasure
3	*The Slavery of Our Times* (1890)	Dialogical self	Pursuance of higher law against lower law; conscience over majoritarianism; against the majoritarianism-based led ethos-based Parliament; rejection of violence; preferring soul force against brute forces
4	*The First Step: An Essay on the Morals of Diet*(1891)	Self-Other	Controlling palate and rejection of consumption-driven being; abstinence from animal food, thus preferring vegetarianism and fasting; the plight of working people linked to consumption of affluent classes

5	*How Shall We Escape (1898)*	Action based on conscience/ consciousness of truth	Against exploiting workers and the working class, refusal to participate in violence
6	*A Letter to a Hindoo* (1908)	Multi-religious pluralism	Satyagraha, disobedience against tyranny, not eye for an eye, modern civilization as a site of violence, non-participation in evil or injustice;
Robert Sherard			
7	*The White Slaves of England* (1897)	Feelings for workers	Indictment of modern civilization for the vulnerable condition of male and female workers
Edward Carpenter			
8	*Civilisation: Its Cause and Cure* (1889)	Health as unity, linking self and other, reconciliation between human and nature, linking logical and intellectual parts of human beings from the emotional instinct, inclusion of other in our life	Civilization as a disease; fault lines concerning Doctors; civilisation as inequality; against the separation between mind and body; law as the morality of ruling classes

Thomas F. Taylor		
9	*The Fallacy of Speed* (1909)	Intertwined local relationships	Analysis of speed and railway, the significance of interdependence, critique of heavy machinery and urbanism
Godfrey Blount			
10	*A New Crusade: An Appeal* (1903)	Country life and handicrafts	Critique of materialism; rejection of over-dependence on machinery and manufacturing towns; rejection of competitive mechanical production
Henry David Thoreau			
11	*On the Duty of Civil Disobedience* (1849)	Conscientious individuals	Satyagraha, resistance to unjust laws, conscience over the state
12	*Life Without Principle* (1863)	Ethical life, moral freedom	
John Ruskin			
13	*Unto This Last* (1862)	Sound of the individual is to the good of all; equal value of all work; valuable life of labour	Putting the idea of equality and equal worthiness into practice against the unjust structures
14	*A Joy for Ever (And Its Price in the Market)* (1857)	Ethical action, meaningful use of wealth	Rejection of morality of money

		Giuseppe Mazzini	
15	*Duties of Man* (1862)	True man, democratic unity, common good, people as sovereign, earth as heaven, preaching virtue-sacrifice-love, higher stage of existence, life by a higher law, association, womens' rights	Capital as want and poverty of multitude; rejection of violence; problematizing governing laws
		Plato	
16	*Defence and Death of Socrates*	Individuals as morally excellent, virtuous, reformer and devoid of fear of death; learning to live and die; the importance of means over money; the importance of soul, wisdom and truth over honour and reputation; strive for perfection, virtue causes wealth not otherwise; the importance of right act;	Fight against the corrupt element or observation of the traditional religion; Satyagrahi/ satyagraha against a disease that is oppressed by the British regime; the problem of judgment by the majority; die for the chosen path; need of a critique, critiquing majoritarianism; justice as a central category, no fear of death, no appealing

		Max Nordau	
17	*The Conventional Lies of Civilization* (1883)	Sovereignty with people not in divine power; republic as the realization of self-government	Critique of civilization discourse; critique of organized religion; critique of inequality, the state; critique of parliamentarism
	Paradox (1886)	People in non-minority or majority category	The rejection of the superficial notion of majority and minority;
		Dadabhai Naoroji	
18	*Poverty and Un-British Rule in India* (1901)	People in the non-exploitative category	Critique of railway, critique of colonization and the rejection of capitalism/imperialism pauperization due to lack of attention, stress on agriculture
		Romesh Chunder Dutt	
19	*Economic History of India.* (Volume I: 1902; Volume II: 1904).	People need non-discriminatory treatment.	The rejection of capitalism/imperialism; pauperization due to lack of attention; stress on agriculture; rejection of railway-centric development
		Henry Summer Maine	
20	*Village communities in the East and West* (1871)	Village communities, customary laws, self-organized groups, commons	Problematic of codified laws

Satyagraha and Sovereignity

Satyagraha makes people sovereign. The people as sovereign encompasses "antagonism" against injustice. This is crucial for the arrival and continuation of swaraj while creating a distinct alternative collective association. Swaraj can be called a political community based on satyagraha for the collective association through developing "antagonism" against injustices. It requires elaboration.

Satyagraha is the defining feature of Gandhian philosophy and action. It introduces a slew of Promethean values in action. The idea of defiance or disobedience against injustice, self-suffering, sacrifice, the openness of action and grievances, the transformation of both oppressed and oppressor, conscience, higher law and lower law and a determination based on truth and non-violence are principles of satyagraha for forming a collective. The collective formed by satyagraha instils the value of these individuals against injustice.[447]

This may look simple, naive or impractical, but this is also the beginning of the turning points in the discourse on the relationship among the state, individuals, disobedience and protest. The relationship was shaped by indigenes, binaries amongst the state and non-state actors and the capital and east–west dichotomy. Since the modern nation-state operates laws or laws considered to be the legitimate will, Gandhi invites attention to this "legitimate will". A foundation of discrimination can also be operated through the legitimate will. For Gandhi, "just will" can be legitimate will, but it is not necessarily the case that "legitimate will" can also be just will.

Against this backdrop, retrieving the "principle of antagonism" becomes crucial. The principle of reconciliation and antagonism are twin principles in Gandhi's schema, which he champions. He applies the principle of reconciliation to beings. At the level of beings, he rejects the principle of antagonism. For Gandhi, people must invent their self by others. Other is the core of one's self. There cannot be self without another. De-selfing is a crucial component. Therefore, violence against others is also violence against the self. The principle of antagonism applies to the governing laws of beings. In the case of injustice or discrimination, the principle of antagonism becomes the ultimate principle.

The principle of antagonism makes people sovereign.

Gandhi's resistance to governing laws of beings is essential due to its *transformative effect*. People are not static or immovable. There is nothing called permanent co-option. If injustice prevails, the relevance and practice of satyagraha continue in a particular way, which is antagonism towards control. In Gandhi's time and the contemporary world, laws are a compelling signpost for deciding, touching and regulating the modus vivendi of human beings.

The principle of antagonism begins with defying unjust laws, which shapes the sovereignty of the swaraj-led political community. The alternative political community is impregnated in satyagraha. In it, there is the birth of a sovereign. The sovereign is the people. Unfortunately, the principles of reconciliation and antagonism are not differentiated in analyses. The latter is also a crucial component for the arrival of swaraj by giving birth to the sovereign.

"Law as command", "law as rule" and inseparability between "law and morality" have been pivotal debates. "Law as command" is about the apotheosis of laws. The idea of positive laws becomes crucial. Positivist laws are laws bereft of moralism. Laws are treated as command and commanded. There is a command theory by the sovereign. The existence of law[448] backed by the command to punish for noncompliance by a sovereign, not obeying anyone else is a feature of positive law.[449] The command implies "sanction" or "enforcement of obedience", "duty" or "obligation", and "superior and inferior".[450] "A Milton or a Hampden might animate their countrymen to resistance, but a Hobbes or a Falkland would counsel obedience and peace."[451] Furthermore, a sovereign becomes significant. "Every positive law, or every law simply and strictly so called, is set by a sovereign person, or a sovereign body of persons, to a member or members of the independent political society wherein that person or body is sovereign or supreme."[452]

There is an assertion for 'law as rules' within positive law schools. The law combines primary rules (rules imposing duties) and secondary rules (power-conferring rules; rules about primary/basic rules). Concerning the primary or basic rules,

> [H]uman beings are required to do or abstain from certain actions, whether they wish to or not. Rules of the other type are in a sense parasitic upon or secondary to the first; for they provide that human beings may by doing or saying certain things introduce new rules of the primary type, extinguish, or modify old ones, or in various ways determine their incidence or control their operations . . . Rules of the first type concern actions involving physical movement or changes; rules of the second type provide for operations which lead not merely to physical movement or change, but to the creation or variation of duties or obligations.[453]

Laws as rules entail the universal application of laws in the positivist sense that they apply to everyone.

Laws as principle and morality are equally crucial. Laws as a principle are emphasised because there is no separation between laws and morality. "Law is effectively integrated with morality: lawyers and judges are working political philosophers of a democratic state."[454] Thus, it is well-accepted that laws cannot be delinked from morality.

However, this discourse has yet to clarify the location of satyagraha/civil disobedience. One position outrightly rejects the possibility of satyagraha. "(1) there is no moral right to civil disobedience in liberal states; (2) normally there is such a right in illiberal states."[455] Moreover, "a state of near justice", "[e]veryone's exercising . . . [civil disobedience] . . . would have deleterious consequences for all".[456] "Thus the exercise of the right to civil disobedience should, like any other right, be rationally framed to advance one's ends or the ends of those one wishes to assist."[457] "So long as the law appears to make acts of dissent criminal, a man of conscience will face danger."[458]

The problem occurs because the notion of sovereignty is defined in res publica rather than as a people. Res publica is an encompassing landscape in which people are treated merely according to *recognized components*. Two possible outlines of Gandhi and political action are outlined.

Firstly, it is related to "moral exemplar".

In Gandhi's writing, there is an implicit but bold proposal: "When one chooses for oneself, *one sets an example to everyone*." That is the role of the satyagrahi. To lead exemplary lives, to set examples for everyone by their actions. The concept of the exemplar is intended to provide a wholesale alternative to the concept of principle in moral philosophy.[459]

Secondly, 'Gandhian political realism' becomes a crucial aspect.

> Although Gandhi is often taken to be an exemplary moral idealist in politics . . . Gandhian non-violence is premised on a form of political realism, specifically a contextual, consequentialist, and moral-psychological analysis of a political world understood to be marked by inherent tendencies toward conflict, domination, and violence . . . The singularity of satyagraha lies in its self-limiting character as a form of political action that seeks to constrain the negative consequences of politics while working toward progressive social and political reform. Gandhian nonviolence thereby points toward a transformational realism that need not begin and end in conservatism, moral equivocation, or pure instrumentalism.[460]

This helps us understand Gandhi's reasoning for his sovereignty. Gandhian sovereignty combines moral exemplar and political action. If the former instils the value of autonomy due to the action's non-duality and the absence of a dichotomy between personal privilege and sacrifice for others, the latter paves the way for transformational politics by concretising actions, avoiding the vagueness of direction of only personal changes.

Taking the argument further, Gandhi's laws and justice must be seen together. Gandhi's earliest belief in the context of South Africa was "that the whole duty of an advocate was not to exploit legal and adversary advantages but to promote compromise and reconciliation."[461] Gandhi studied and practised law for twenty-three years (1888–1911). Gandhi's civil disobedience has the following features: "honouring one's conscience", "testing the law", "advancing the debate" and "creating change".[462]

Honouring one's conscience: While much civil disobedience has multiple motives, a disobedient might defy the law principally for reasons of conscience.

Testing the law: Often the quickest—and in some circumstances the only—way to get a ruling on the validity of a law is to break the law and thus force a criminal prosecution of the disobedient. In that event, a forum is created for the disobedient to mount his or her argument in a court against the validity of the law as part of the disobedient's defence.

Advancing the debate: When public discussion of a vital issue is stagnant or non-existent, civil disobedience can cause discussion to further develop or to arise for the first time. A disobedient's act, if sufficiently out of the ordinary and sufficiently open, attracts the attention of the media and the public. Debate on the substantive issue often follows.

Creating change: Civil disobedience can be used to create various forms of change—political, social, cultural, legal and more. It does so through what is now a fairly well-established dynamic. The disobedient breaks a law; the disobedient suffers; the public takes note of the suffering and inquires as to the reason for the disobedient's action; the public sympathizes with the disobedient; the public puts pressure for change on those in power; and those in power react by enacting curative, institutional reform.[463]

Conscience to change is a critical component of people as sovereign.

In Gandhi's case, positivist laws are rejected because they delink morality from laws. This is a critical component for the arrival of people as sovereigns. Laws, as a rule, give way to laws as a principle, which is also a Dworkinian position. Laws as principles come closer to morality. It is stated that it is a "moral obligation to disobey law" in case of unjust laws.[464] Equally, the "political" in Gandhi needs to be highlighted. In other words, Gandhi's sovereign is both moral and political, i.e. moral as political and political as moral.

In classical studies on "political", "political" is a binary between friend and enemy.[465] Political is also "antagonistic pluralism".[466] It is crucial to understand the distinction

> ... between "the political" and "politics." [Political refers] ... to the dimension of antagonism that is inherent in all human society, antagonism that can take many different forms and can emerge in diverse social relations. "Politics," on the other hand, refers to the ensemble of practices, discourses and institutions that seek to establish a certain order and to organize human coexistence in conditions that are always potentially conflictual because they are affected by the dimension of "the political." It is only when we acknowledge this dimension of "the political" and understand that "politics" consists in domesticating hostility, only in trying to defuse the potential antagonism that exists in human relations, that we can pose the fundamental question for democratic politics.[467]

In the backdrop of two types of political relations (antagonism between enemies; agonism between adversaries), It can be stated

. . . that the aim of democratic politics is to transform an "antagonism" into an "agonism". This has important consequences for the way we envisage politics. Contrary to the model of "deliberative democracy", the model of "agonistic pluralism" . . . asserts that the prime task of democratic politics is not to eliminate passions nor to relegate them to the private sphere in order to render rational consensus possible, but to mobilise those passions towards the promotion of democratic designs. Far from jeopardizing democracy, agonistic confrontation is in fact its very condition of existence.[468]

Gandhi's notable contribution concerns combining moral and political values while developing reconciliation at the level of beings and antagonism towards injustice. At the being level, he rules out even agonism, but antagonism remains a powerful principle concerning unjust laws or injustice. Gandhi's politics unravel the contradictions of satyagraha in specific ways. Satyagraha is a non-violent resistance. Gandhi asserts that satyagraha is soul force, truth force and love force. The first part of each (soul, truth, love) denotes the reconciliation of beings subject to a slew of discrimination. The second part denotes antagonism towards unjust governing laws or structures. It is the quest for the principle of life.

A good man will therefore resist an evil system or administration with his whole soul. Disobedience of the law of an evil State is therefore a duty. Violent disobedience deals with men who can be replaced. It leaves the evil itself untouched and often accentuates it. Nonviolent, i.e., civil disobedience is the only and the most successful remedy and is obligatory upon him who would dissociate himself from evil.[469]

Gandhi emphasizes linking law and conscience. "If I find that even my father has imposed upon me a law which is repugnant to my conscience, I think it is the least drastic course that I could adopt by respectfully telling him that I cannot obey it."[470] He further links it with the inherent rights of citizens, which does not lead to anarchy. "Civil Disobedience is the inherent right of a citizen . . . Civil Disobedience is never followed by anarchy."[471] Moreover, "[c]ivil Disobedience, therefore, becomes a sacred duty when the state has become lawless, or which is the same thing, corrupt."[472]

This is how Gandhi prepares people as sovereigns for swaraj. It can be further elaborated on with two different notions of society.

The prevalent method is "we want a just society". This method unravels the idea of a political community without solving existing contradictions. In it, the principle of reconciliation, which ideally should operate at the level of beings, is extended to the governing laws of humans. This makes the absence of political. Therefore, laws embody the principle of reconciliation. On the other hand, "we do not want an unjust society" is the alternative principle. In it, or Gandhian justice, unjust laws are problematized. Justice is linked with *sarvodaya*. It can be called the anti-metaphysical alternative principle. This can be called the principle of antagonism. Gandhi engages laws as political in terms of highlighting antagonism, not reconciliation. Reconciliation avoids the idea of justice, whereas the Gandhian notion of "antagonism" embodies the idea of justice. In other words, Gandhi's ideas of politics are based on antagonism, which rejects unjust laws based on reconciliation in the domain of institutions.

Gandhi divides laws into two categories, i.e., higher laws and lower laws. In fact, higher laws also include the idea of justice, whereas lower laws are mere laws which are positive laws. His notion of satyagraha is linked to *sarvodaya* or *antodaya*. For Gandhi, *sarvodaya*, deriving from Ruskin's *Unto This Last*, is as follows: "That the good of the individual is contained in the good of all."[473] This is also a rejection of utilitarian laws.

In *Hind Swaraj*, Chapter 17 is crucial, which is on passive resistance. Gujarati and Hindi editions titled it *Satyagraha.*:

> A man who has realized his manhood, who fears only God, will fear no one else. Man-made laws are not necessarily binding on him. Even the Government does not expect any such thing from us. They do not say: "You must do such and such a thing," but they say: "If you do not do it, we will punish you." We are sunk so low that we fancy that it is our duty and our religion to do what the law lays down. If man will only realize that it is unmanly to obey laws that are unjust, no man's tyranny will enslave him. This is the key to self-rule or home-rule.[474]

Gandhi takes the debate further from laws and obedience. He converts people into sovereigns who resist tyranny or tyrannical laws. People, as sovereign, do not regard unjust commands. ". . . [T]he commands of the rulers do not go beyond the point of their swords, for true men disregard unjust commands."[475]

His statement in a court during Champaran Satyagraha (1917) (*Written Statement filed by M.K. Gandhi before Subdivisional Magistrate, Motihari, on 18 April 1917, in response to Notice, U/S 144, Cr. P.C)*[476] asserted the supremacy of a higher law.

> I venture to make this statement not in any way in extenuation of the penalty to be awarded against me, but to show that I

have disregarded the order served upon me not for want of respect for lawful authority, but in obedience to the higher law of our being, the voice of conscience.[477]

Gandhi wrote three articles responsible for 'The Great Trial of Gandhi' in 1922 and, subsequently, his "The Great Trial Speech"(1922). These three articles are "Tempering with Loyalty" (*Young India*, 29 September 1921), "The Puzzle and Its Solution" (*Young India*, 15 December 1921) and "Shaking the Manes" (*Young India*, 23 February 1922). Some excerpts are telling statements.

"Tempering with Loyalty" (*Young India*, 29 September 1921):

The Conference at Karachi merely repeated the Congress declaration in terms of Islam . . . but speaking for Hinduism and speaking for nationalism I have no hesitation in saying that it is sinful for anyone, either as soldier or civilian, to serve this Government which has proved treacherous to the Mussalmans of India and which had been guilty of the inhumanities of the Punjab.[478]

"A Puzzle and Its Solution" (*Young India*, 15 December 1921):

We desire to show that the Government exists to serve the people, not the people the Government.[479]

"Shaking the Manes" (*Young India*, 23 February 1922):

The rice-eating puny millions of India seem to have resolved upon achieving their own destiny without any further tutelage and without.

I am aware that I have written strongly about the insolent threat that has come from across the seas, but it is high time that the British people were made to realise that the fight that was commenced in 1920 is a fight to the finish, whether it lasts one month or one year or many months or many years, and whether the representatives of Britain re-enact all the indescribable orgies of the Mutiny days with redoubled force or whether they do not.[480]

At the Circuit House at Shahi Bag, the trial of Mr Gandhi and Mr Banker commenced on Saturday noon, 18 March, before Mr C. N. Broomsfield, G. S., District and Sessions Judge of Ahmedabad. Gandhi, in his introductory remarks before reading his statement, said, "The only course open to you, the Judge, is, as I am just going to say in my statement, either to resign your post, or inflict on me the severest penalty, if you believe that the system and law you are assisting to administer are good for the people."[481] In the statement, inter alia, he advocated for the right to expression of the non-violent nature of disaffection. "Affection cannot be manufactured or regulated by law. If one has no affection for a person or system, one should be free to give the fullest expression to his disaffection, so long as he does not contemplate, promote or incite to violence."[482]

In the aforesaid statements and remarks, Gandhi offers "democratic nonviolent antagonism". There is a rejection of positivist laws. Questioning laws is one of the cornerstones of satyagraha. Laws as a principle must be prioritized over laws as a rule. He combines laws and justice together. Herein, laws are meaningless sans injustice. Justice is higher laws based on the rejection of violence, and violence is asymmetrical relations based on caste, class, gender and communalism.

This is the birth and reassertion of a sovereign who also changes the nature of political obedience and political obligation.

"Political obligation" envisages a political association for the fulfilment of realizing self-perfection. Rights cannot exist without association or civic institutions, thus creating the concept of political obligation. It is for our benefit to follow political obligation.[483]

There is a problematization of liberal political theory or liberal democracy because, in the name of political obligation, there is political obedience. In fact, political obedience is practised while promising voluntarism, which cannot be fulfilled. "The consent is political fiction" in liberal democracy. The promise of the future is obtained in political obedience. Only in democratic theory is political obligation possible, which means everyday democracy and participation. Political education in place of political socialisation is proposed.[484] "One reason why the identification of 'consent' and 'democracy' with liberal democracy is so rarely challenged is that 'many people are linguistically inhibited from thinking theoretically about politics'. They are neither taught nor encouraged to think in a critical and systematic way about their relationship to the liberal democratic state . . . "[485] Moreover, civic virtue and cooperative enterprise are also envisaged against the theory of incompatibility between autonomy and authority.[486] "For people to think of obeying the law as an instance of the cooperation that preserves a cooperative enterprise, they must first think of themselves as citizens or members who have an obligation to their fellow citizens or members to obey. They must think of themselves, that is, as participants in a cooperative enterprise."[487]

Gandhi's "antagonism" changes the contour of political obedience for the arrival of participatory democracy. In his notion of sarvodaya, political obligation is a self-reflective endeavour. In the Gandhian schema, satyagraha, as the principle of antagonism against unjust governing laws, is conjoined by an emphasis on "extra-parliamentary" through the constructive programme. If satyagraha enables people to be sovereign, the constructive programme brings attention to this sovereign and the massive prevailing contradiction in society.

Gandhi confronted two crucial gaps in liberal political theory or institutions. The first was the problem of definite space. The idea of laws and injustice is recognized only through a definite space of politics. The second is constrained representation. Laws and justice are guided by the approval of constrained representation by way of logic of representation. In this way, law and justice become a very privileged notion, available to only a few, despite the idea of due legitimation.

Gandhi explores laws and justice beyond the definite space and constrained justice in which real justice could be delivered. These are the spaces where both antagonism and justice need to be delivered. In the *Constructive Programme*, Gandhi could identify eighteen such spaces for the principle of antagonism to deliver sarvodaya's notion of justice.[488] It can be expanded further in the case of identification of injustices.

Gandhi's satyagraha offers the notion of people as sovereign, which is reconciliatory at the level of being but antagonistic at governing the unjust laws of human beings. Satyagraha makes the arrival of people as sovereign feasible. This sovereign is crucial for achieving and sustaining the values of swaraj.

Swaraj without people as sovereign is an unthinkable and unachievable apotheosis. People, as sovereigns, are the chief anchor of *Hind Swaraj*.

People as sovereigns are unique in that they are intertwined between political action and sovereignty. Gandhi offers a "non-Weberian" notion of the state (the state has the supreme right to the legitimacy of the violence) where the centre is not located in *res publica* but in people, while there is no question of allowing the condition for violence. 'Exception to non-violence' is ruled out in the Weberian state. Gandhi restores the normalcy to non-violence through people as sovereign, which operates through "no exception to violence".

Alternative Political Community[489]

In addition to other significant sources, Gandhi's suggestions of twenty books (plus one) shaped the contours of *Hind Swaraj.* The text underlies the importance of satyagraha. It offers the principle of antagonism against unjust laws. In this way, swaraj becomes a political community while deliberating on twenty metaphors.

In other words, the way towards an alternative political community involves making people sovereign, embracing the principle of reconciliation and embracing the principle of antagonism. The principle of antagonism activates ontological reminders of the political community.

Gandhi's political community is based on *ontological reminder.* The ontological reminder entails associational norms. Associational norms ask questions about why and how we are associated. The ontological reminder is different from *ontological indifference.* Ontological indifference is based on governing norms in which people are *subject* to the state and government. In this way, Gandhi offers swaraj as a political community in which interdependence is significant. In other words, swaraj is an interdependent relation. It problematizes dependent relations, which cause exploitation, humiliation and alienation. It makes people a central category for reminding the association norms.

Reading twenty chapters of *Hind Swaraj* as metaphors of the political community needs some clarification. Metaphors are essential underneath the comprehensive outline. Metaphors contain cognitive value. They cannot be rejected as being dubbed as an expression of dynamic value. Metaphors must not be read literally. There must be an exercise of reading beyond words. They constitute concepts and are not simply ornamental expressions. Since they have temporal locations, it becomes crucial to be acquainted with them later to understand the meaning of the former. Metaphors are not beyond socio-economic realities. They are substantive expressions of it.

Reading *Hind Swaraj* along these lines, the meaning must be extended by words. Gandhi formulates definite concepts containing cognitive and epistemic values. These are not simply or merely emotional outbursts or rejection of imperialism. It cannot be reduced to literal rigidities.

"The Congress and Its Officials" invite attention to *seeking equivalence over benevolence*. Gandhi rejects petitioning and adopts struggle. Struggle offers equivalence status while rejecting pity and passivity (Chapter One). "The Partition of Bengal" helps us understand "awakening". Awakening becomes the *sine qua non* for the realization of swaraj. It is also a rejection of the method of petitioning (Chapter Two). "Discontent and Unrest" underlie that discontent is necessary for awakening. Discontent precedes awakening, awakening from slumber and conditionalities (Chapter Three). "What is swaraj?" offers both negation and transformation. It rejects what swaraj is not. It cannot be mere political independence but structural transformation (Chapter Four).

"The Condition of England" abjures delegation. People's sovereignty cannot be delegated. Delegation circumvents the political self, which is *thinking politically*, i.e., self-ruling internally and externally (Chapter Five). "Civilisation" is to be interpreted as a rejection of modern civilization, which is based on exclusivism. Gandhi offers an alternative in the form of true civilization beyond the "modern civilization" formulation (Chapter Six). "Why was India Lost?" invites attention towards responsibility. We are responsible for our actions. Therefore, activating agency and the significance of satyagraha is essential (Chapter Seven). "The Condition of India" proposes realizing "ethical cosmopolitanism". He redefines the usage and meaning of religion by proposing religion as the realization of self. Self-realization of each other paves the way for dialogical integration (Chapter Eight).

"Railway" represents an "uncontrolled" dimension or uncontrolled exploitation. It also points out that *speed* is an uncontrolled entity, which means people are part of political control without control of it. The political community is an uncontrolled dimension to them (Chapter Nine). "The Hindus and the Mohammedans" offer the metaphor of an *alter ego*. It breaks the binaries between the two and circumvents the possibility of an empirical majority deciding their relationship. Gandhi recognizes the difference in existence but rules out separation (Chapter Ten). "Lawyers" emphasize the *negation of arbitration*. He suggests it happens through the practice of profiting over justice. Arbitration does not solve problems but aggravates them (Chapter Eleven). "Doctors" problematize the "appearance over essence" position. His difference between disease and deed is remarkable. His appeals beyond physiological are worthy of highlighting socio-economic complexities (Chapter Twelve).

In "What Is True Civilisation?", Gandhi interprets good conduct as inclusivism. Gandhi used political philosophy over history. Civilization claims that inclusivism is a normative positing against imperialism or binarism (Chapter Thirteen). "How Can India Become Free?" proposes transcendence. Freedom in Gandhi is transcendence. Here, both individual and structure presuppose freedom. There cannot be free individuals in unfree structures (Chapter Fourteen). "Italy and India" ponders over the rejection of teleology. He questions his condition. There is nothing good in one's own and villainous in others teleologically. Teleological order is brute force. Gandhi rejects the structural foundation of violence and brutality and its promises, i.e., *it is designed permanently*. Self cannot be violently predestined. It cannot be subsumed under the control of others. This is brute force. It is teleological, which must be rejected (Chapter Fifteen). "Brute Force" calls for the significance of deontology. He rejects the distinction between means and ends and the utilitarian principle. His ethical means include both principle (normativity of values) and political act (assertion of values). Both are crucial for defining the outcome. In the fight against unjust orders and laws, one cannot compromise on either because the result cannot be just (Chapter Sixteen).

"Passive Resistance" is the truth force for negating brute force. *Satyagraha* is a crucial canon for sustaining the nature of the political community. It rejects, confirms, and affirms the activation of the agency. Obeying the unethical state violates truth and non-violence (Chapter Seventeen). "Education" entails communicative action. Education cannot be a fetish. It is undiluted learning. There is no distinction between intellectual education and learning a craft. The mother tongue becomes crucial to knowing the surroundings. This is important to conclude sans violence.

Moreover, communication action becomes crucial for the arrival of swaraj by way of satyagraha (Chapter Eighteen). "Machinery" is a metaphor for exploitation. Technology is exploitative because it enslaves humans. It is a hindrance. It also harms people politically or thinking politically, thus causing them to be unaware of contradictions (Chapter Nineteenth). "Conclusion" envisages a future without violence and petition. In Gandhi's case, violence and petitioning remain problematic components. Swaraj is without violence and petitioning (Chapter Twenty).

Redefining the Notion of Swaraj

Gandhi offers a distinct notion of swaraj. Swaraj may be defined in six distinguished ways. Firstly, it can be called the continuation of the ancient notion in which "abstract engagement" is hypothesized. The concept here is not considered a new contribution. It is just a rephrasing of the past concept in modern times. In abstract engagement, a concept is considered doing an *act* with the minimum definition of the concept. The control of *swa* (self) is the sublimity of one's composed condition. The assumption of *swa* through control becomes the deciding factor over the act of the *self*. Secondly, swaraj is also interpreted as self-government where "own people" constitute a ruling. Herein, the debates about res publics as an ultimate signpost of sovereignty become the most important reference and assertion point. Autonomy is defined in a territorial sense. Thirdly, swaraj is asserted in the realm of ideas. Here, indigenism is both assertive and universal. The rejection of "the outside epistemic resource" becomes the focal point. Whole and parts of swaraj are defined in indigenous episteme in which specificity becomes the most important for a universal purpose. Fourthly, swaraj is also defined in the sense of religious supremacy. The *swa* is defined as *us* versus *them*. 'Us' is religious superiority. It is a definite delineation and categorical superiority. Religion is defined as cultural superiority. In this case, religion as a cultural superiority gives a distinct identity. The swa and swaraj become apotheosis of distinctiveness. Fifthly, cultural superiority, therefore, is translated into political aggrandisement. There cannot be swaraj in cultural superiority without political processes. The religious episteme shapes individuals and society. The political process does two things. It constitutes the subject of religious episteme and shaping the policies of res publica.

His rejection principle and alternative principle are categorical about swaraj. His rejection principle rejects swaraj as an abstract assumption where the concept is itself acting. It is not composed of status through control. Swaraj is also not just owned by its own people for mere *territorial suzerainty*. Swaraj is also not just an idea or ideational state for sublimity. Swaraj is not simply an epistemological supremacy. It also cannot be religious supremacy. Since he rejects swaraj as cultural supremacy, the political aggrandisement associated with it is also rejected. Gandhi's swaraj significantly differs from the swaraj discourse given above. The alternative principle in Gandhi makes satyagraha a way of achieving swaraj. Change is needed by ruling out the concept and practice of the enemy. Gandhi rejects the possibility of political theology based on friend and enemy. His satyagraha gives birth to people as sovereigns who constitute the swaraj. Herein, collectivity and interdependence become the supreme value. Gandhi's swaraj offers epistemic diversity, non-binary politics and others as the most essential constituent of the self.

The critique of modern civilization asserts that people are sovereign for the interdependent political community that is swaraj.